EDUCATION
FOR A NEW WORLD ORDER

J S Rajput

Published by
Renu Kaul Verma
Vitasta Publishing Pvt Ltd
4348/4C, Ansari Road, Daryaganj
New Delhi-110 002
info@vitastapublishing.com

ISBN: 978-81-19670-61-1
© J S Rajput
First Edition 2024
MRP ₹ 495

All Rights Reserved.
No part of this publication may be reproduced, stored in a retrieval system, or transmitted in any form, or by any means – electronic, mechanical, photocopying, recording or otherwise – without the prior permission of the publisher.

Edited by Indu Ramchandani
Typeset & Cover Design by Somesh Kumar Mishra
Printed by Vikas Computer and Printers, New Delhi

Contents

Introduction   *vii*

Chapter 1 Our Glorious Heritage   **1-39**
The Concept of Dharma   3
Swami Vivekananda's Vision for Education   7
Mahatma Gandhi on Education in India   13
Rabindranath Tagore's Vision of Education   21
Focus on Indigenous Education   27
Upheaval at the Advent of the 20th Century   31
Basic Elements of Interfaith Education   32
Today's Perspective   35
The Post-Independence Era   37
Onward Journey   38

Chapter 2 Global Educational Scenario and Emerging Trends   **40-56**
Global Educational Change and the Indian Context   42

Sustainable Development	42
Reformulate Education for Sustainable Development	43
World Conference on Education for All (WCEFA)	47
Delors Commission Report of 1996	48
Education for a Sustainable World	53
Human Development versus Environment	54

Chapter 3 Transforming Higher Education: Directions and Possibilities   57-89

Education for Learning to Live Together	59
Educational Institutions Must Look Within	61
The Ethos of Quality Erosion in Education	62
A Case Study	64
Equality of Opportunity and Talent Nurturance	67
Education for Civil Behaviour	70
Education Must Acculturate	73
Elements of Educational Change	76
Revitalising Distraught Education Systems	81
Building Educational Institutions	85

Chapter 4 Higher Education: Vision, Growth, and Governance   90-108

The Background of a Rich Heritage	90
From Social Support to State Control	91
Post-Independence Growth in Education	92
The Turbulent Trajectory of the Education System	95
Current State of Disarray	97
The On-going Challenge	97

Preparing for the Emerging Scenario	99
National Education Policy	101
Academic Leadership	102
Percept to Practice	103
A Case for Case Studies	104
The Task Ahead	106

Chapter 5 Transformative Education and Education Policies — **109-131**

The Emerging Indian Education System — NEP 2020	110
Transformational Reforms	112
Global Context of the National Education Policy	114
Syllabus Reduction	117
Revising Textbooks	122
The Issue of Medium of Instruction	125
Basic Education and the New Education Policy	128
Teachers and the National Education Policy	129

Chapter 6 Inculcating Research Culture in the Learning Process — **132-143**

Motivation	134
Research is a Cautious Quest	136
Evaluating Research	138

Chapter 7 Covid-19 and Its Impact — **144-149**

Chapter 8 Digital Transformation of Education Systems — **150-157**

On-line Studies	151
The Digital Wave	153

Chapter 9 Towards Transformational Reforms in Education for Vision 2047   **158-174**

Action Plan and Document on Vision India@2047   158

Education during the Covid-19 Pandemic   162

NEP 2020 Implementation from 2021-2023   164

Implementation of NEP through Consultation and Collaboration   168

NEP 2020 Implementation Challenges   171

The Way Forward   173

Bibliography   *175*

Introduction

Education is universally accepted as the 'ray of hope' for everyone, particularly for those forced to remain in the 'back rows' for generations in the social, economic, cultural context. The debilitating impact of several such discriminations has been acknowledged and numerous initiatives have been launched to ensure human dignity to one and all, irrespective of any diversity of caste, colour, race, region, or religion. Education for all is the most potent strategy to overcome the clouds of ignorance, superstition, and inhuman discrimination that have engulfed the lives of millions for ages. The decade of the 20th century gave great impetus to the global efforts to attain the goal of universal elementary education. Although the target is yet to be achieved, global literacy is now above 84 per cent, which is very promising. Education policies have already moved far ahead from offering only literacy and numeracy to ensuring good quality education integrated with skill acquisition, and along with that promise, comprehensive growth and personality development for every individual.

Education is the fundamental human right of everyone without any discrimination due to any social, cultural, religious, economic, and racial diversity. In a fast-changing world, every individual deserves multi-faceted development of all of the five domains of human personality: physical, intellectual, emotional, psychological, and spiritual. These are the major contributors in determining the objectives of education in terms of acquiring knowledge, skill, balance, vision, and identity. Human understanding of the forces of nature has enhanced manifold during the last ten to twelve decades, and it is indeed intriguing that human beings have self-inflicted disastrous results on humanity, leading to serious concerns on the very existence of Planet Earth and life on it! Human existence today confronts conflict, tension, hatred, distrust, violence, and war all around.

After WWII, especially after the annihilation of the atom bombs, concerted efforts were made to create global platforms such as the UN and UNESCO to encourage dialogue and deliberations to banish wars and violence, hunger and poverty forever, from the face of earth. But ironically, the World Wars did not put an end to wars and skirmishes around the world. Therefore, the goal, yet unreached, appears far more elusive at this juncture than it did some eight decades ago. Practically every country is facing crises of the ideology of progress, economic crisis, and to a great extent, some sort of moral crisis. There could be many such crises at diverse national levels. Significant demographic changes in several countries have resulted in serious social, cultural, linguistic, and religious conflicts. As things are becoming more and more complex, education policies are being examined very seriously by practically every nation. After several attempts at developing a comprehensive Education Policy, India devoted four years to arrive at its National Education Policy of 2020 (NEP-2020). This Policy, apart from unprecedented level and numbers of consultations, has drawn heavily from post-Independence experiential learning and a futuristic assessment of the world emerging as it is, for the twenty-first century generation. The essential spirit and intent of the policy meant for decades ahead, has reached all concerned, and the transformation has begun in all sincerity and commitment. Impediments of the lack of resources and inadequacies in manpower are aspects that need sustained efforts and inputs.

The emerging scenario is not bereft of major challenges, but offers unprecedented opportunities and opens up numerous avenues for intellectual adventure, comprehension of social and emotional aspects of learning, continuous skill acquisition and development of new skills, and enthusiasm towards innovations. India shares the universally accepted premise that new education must be rooted in the culture and life of the people, and simultaneously must open routes to new knowledge. The mobility of intellectuals and innovators in this global 'village' must increase manifold, the number of collaborative initiatives in every sector must also grow, and at every level, qualified persons with diverse backgrounds need to be working together. It would be imperative on every active and alert citizen to delineate his or her role in helping to combat the major global crises such as climate change, air pollution, water, food shortage and help in other such sectors, which are proving increasingly detrimental to life itself. Familiarity with issues and concerns listed among the seventeen sustainable development goals SDG-17 is essential, in appropriate form and format, from the very initial stages in education. Seven tensions as listed by the Delores Commission very aptly represent the scenario ahead for present and future generations: tension between global and local, universal and individual, traditional and modern, long-term and short-term considerations, and in the need for competition and the concern for equality of opportunity. In addition, there is tension between the extraordinary expansion of knowledge and the capacity of human beings to assimilate, apart from tension between the spiritual and the material.

An incisive analysis of all seven requires articulation of strategies to reduce, if not eliminate so as to ensure a world of peace with nations that accept the collective responsibility of sustaining the sensitive man-nature relationship. Towards evolving such a strategy, much help and insight flowed from the seven social sins that Mahatma Mohandas Gandhi identified and published in *Young India* of 22 October 1925, and are eternally relevant: politics without principles, wealth without work, pleasure without conscience, knowledge without character, commerce without morality, science without humanity, and worship without sacrifice. While pondering over this 7 X 7 matrix, in which the two sevens may appear disconnected, the fact remains these are strong statements of the problem and also of the solution.

The way out could probably be contained in recalling and comprehending why ancient philosophers of India preferred a duty-based society in place of a rights-based society! Its essence is summarized in one sentence: 'If everyone performs his duty, no one would be denied his right.' Article 51-A on fundamental duties, introduced in the Constitution of India through the 42nd Amendment, could contribute significantly if the sense of duty and debt to parents and family, to knowledge makers and creators, and to nature are fully assimilated and internalised appropriately in the process of teaching and learning. On a broader canvas, austerity, self-restraint, adherence to social needs and readiness to ensure that no one is violated by anyone will make tremendous contribution in national development, social cohesion, and religious amity. These objectives can provide a sound base for curriculum developers and writers of textual materials.

Increase in population demands new schools and universities. Public sector investment in education is seriously stressed. It has impacted the credibility of *sarkari* (government) schools and State-funded universities. People are drifting towards private schools for obvious reasons. Although the two Covid-19 pandemic-hit years (2020-2021) saw some reversal of the trend, private initiative in education will gain greater ground in future.

The difference in quality and credibility both in school education and higher education remains a big challenge in an intensely competitive world that has its own demands of quality, character, dexterity, ideas, imagination, curiosity, creativity, adventure, and innovation. In whichever part of India, a young person receives his higher education, he must be prepared to learn to live together, work together, and achieve together with co-workers of widely varied backgrounds. Renewing existing skills and the readiness to acquire new skills shall gain greater relevance in the world of education and would depend on people's readiness and willingness to learn.

The four stages of the ancient Indian knowledge system continue to remain profoundly relevant even in these years of mesmerising digital learning and the emerging digital pedagogy. These are:

- Acquiring knowledge from parents and teachers.
- Pondering over it; acquiring more on your own and improving upon it.
- Discussing with others; imparting value-added education to others/peers, and later on as parent to your children.
- Using the knowledge so acquired for the benefit of family, society, and for the welfare of all.

Patanjali had advised that everyone has to engage in continuing education throughout life and expand on knowledge. Researchers and innovators are, in fact, paying back the debt to all those who discovered and created knowledge, put it to right use, and we are now enjoying its fruits at present. The process of the expression and utilisation of knowledge requires greater support and autonomy to institutions to enable them to continue with vigour and enthusiasm in institutions of higher learning. A true researcher or scientist studies nature because he or she takes pleasure in it; and that is so because it is beautiful. This is in sharp contrast to the widely prevalent expectation that education must lead to higher incomes and status. When institutions begin to accept this short-sighted goal, the basic objectives of education in transforming a raw, innocent and unaware 'person into a personality' is altogether defeated. Could education achieve such a huge attitudinal transformation on a global scale?

Dynamic education policies in the future shall have to compulsorily comprehend the impact of fast-changing scenarios in every sector. These would need to assess the impact of information and communication technology (ICT) and artificial intelligence (AI), which would also continuously change the very face of the education endeavour. The teacher-education scenario and format would correspondingly also undergo drastic changes in the future. In efforts to adequately equip institutions for the unprecedented changes ahead, the top priority must go towards transformation of teacher-training institutions. Once these institutions present the correct picture of human conduct, character, work culture, empathy, and consideration, their impact could flow to schools, to children, and then to different avocations.

This book attempts to delineate the interdependence of various factors and facets of teaching and learning on the one hand, and projects the emerging aspirations and impediments on the other. It deals with aspects that would form the backbone of the envisaged educational transformation and would indeed accelerate the process if given proper attention and support.

The personal conduct, approach, attitude, and commitment of the teacher are the eternal pivots of value-based humanistic personality development of the learner. The hope is that education systems, including institutions and teachers, and management systems shall work with the conviction that they are creating the future of humanity. Teachers shall remain the 'heart of the learning processes even in the age of ICT and AI. Indian tradition expresses it in profound terms: *Gururgurutamo Dhamah*, meaning the Guru leads from humanity to divinity. Let that be the goal.

The work of this nature requires support and inputs in varied ways from so many learned ones that it is impossible to express gratitude to them and mention them by name. Considerable encouragement came from eminent educationist, Professor P.B. Sharma, Vice Chancellor, Amity

University, Gurgaon, and former President of the Association of Indian Universities; editorial support came from Ms Indu Ramchandani, editorial consultant and Dr Diksha Rajput for her inputs on the implementation of NEP-2020; they deserve a very special mention.

J S Rajput

Chapter 1

Our Glorious Heritage

Education tradition in ancient India had grown around the inherent traits of curiosity, creativity, imagination, ideation, intuition, the capacity to think, and the instinct to explore the secrets of nature. The quest was for in-depth knowledge, not merely the acquiring of information. It was not confined only to the external world. The meaningful education system prepared us to look within, to make an honest effort to comprehend the fuller and larger meaning of life and to ponder on before-life and after-life. And that entire endeavour led to the evolution of human-to-human relationship, and individual-to-nature relationship. The contemplation of the people of our ancient civilisation was deep enough to let them internalise spirituality, human values, and find the best and most satisfying way of life. We also get an insight into how and why Indian civilisation advanced far ahead of others in comprehending the basics of human existence on Earth, queries on life, and on before and after life! If we could correctly comprehend the import of these three aspects, we would naturally be at peace! And that would give greater opportunity and eligibility for more intensive explorations. Logically, the system evolved and was recognised as the unique spiritual advancement of ancient Indian civilisation. Apart from being the inheritors of a great tradition of the quest of knowledge, our literature and scriptures in several languages were great ancient treasures of wisdom and scholarship.

Man's most precious possession is life. Indian tradition eulogises the oneness of *Atman* and *Parmatman*. From that emerges respect for all forms of life. Consequently, respect is inherent to animals, birds, reptiles, trees, plants, vegetation, and marine life. Ancient Indian culture, its scriptures and traditions, accord divinity not only to every human soul but also to birds, animals, trees, mountains, and all that exists as His creation. Man-nature mutuality has been extensively and emphatically described in the scriptures, clearly mentioning that it is man's responsibility to maintain this sensitive link. The scenario so established presents an inspiring ambience to comprehend the essential unity of human beings. The Ancient Indian Theory of Evolution—*Dasha-avatara*—manifests the continuity of the cycle of life. It is tough even for rationalists and well-meaning scientists to ignore it. As one looks beyond the Indian concept, the man being *Amritasya Putra*, child of God, one finds different religious and cultural traditions that articulate the nature of man, his responsibility and his connection with the Almighty. Zoroastrianism declares, 'The Wise One created man to be like Him'; Jains realises the symphony it creates in sync with their tradition when they say, 'Man is creation of God, made in the likeness of God'. In Sikhism, 'God is the Soul of Man, His eternal nature', which appears to reverberate in Christianity's assertion, 'Man is God's workman on earth'.

Does it sound much different from the Islamic contention: 'Man is God's viceroy on earth'? A very pragmatic and inspiring description comes from Confucianism: 'Heaven has made man good, His original nature is good....' Even these simple, rather peripheral descriptions, would indicate very clearly that man has the potential to move towards perfection.

The Concept of *Dharma*

Every parent-teacher today needs to re-learn the importance of the term, *Dharma*—in order to assimilate the ancient Indian tradition of knowledge quest, and comprehend the meaning of *panthnirpekshata* as espoused in the great Indian scriptures. In the Constitution's preamble for 'secularism', (which means equality of all religions), *panthnirpekshata* means equality of all sects.

The term provides the basis for whatever followed in medieval and modern times. The *Vedas*, including the *Upanishads*, as also the *Bhagavad Gita*, the *Mahabharata*, and *Bhagvatam* are the source of *Dharma*, that encompasses all duties and rights that must be strictly adhered to and followed consciously by everyone to ensure a contented, creative, and happy life for all individuals and also for society. The continuity of the comprehension of *Dharma*—which has no equivalent at least in the English language is relevant to a quote from a Judgement of the Supreme Court of India:

> The word Dharma denotes upholding, supporting, nourishing that which upholds, nourishes or supports the stability of the society, maintaining the social order and general well-being and progress of mankind. Whatever conduces to the fulfilment of these objectives is Dharma. *Dharma* is that which your consciousness approves of

and springs from due deliberations for one's own happiness and also for the welfare of all beings free from fear, desire, disease, cherishing good feelings and sense of brotherhood. (In the case of *A.S. Narayana Dixitutlu vs. State of Andhra Pradesh* in 1996).

One wonders why the Indian education system remains shy of clearly taking responsibility to acquaint children and young persons about ancient Indian scriptures, the meaning of *Dharma* that pleads for equality of all human beings irrespective of any conceivable diversity. Why should the system not prepare teachers who understand the Indian tradition of exploring the relationship between man and nature as the salient aspects of spirituality? The basic cultural, social, and humanistic values cherished by Indian civilisation since Vedic times consistently strive to give every human being a dignified life and create conditions and a social environment that offers ample opportunity to develop talents and creativity to the fullest. In this process, every attempt to know the Self, and prepare in life to serve others is one common aspect that becomes part of the *Dharma* of each individual. The ancient Indian scriptures, the source of the knowledge quest tradition, have clearly shown the way to achieve collective aspirations and transformation by all. This is so well illustrated in the Mahabharata:

> The conquest of the self leads to forgiveness and reconciliation, to patience, nonviolence, an attitude of equality, to truth, to simplicity of character, to control over one's physical senses, gentleness, modesty, generosity, to freedom from anger, to a feeling of contentment, pleasant speech, and not seeking fault in others. These are manifestations of conquest over the self.

Only a thoughtfully designed education system, can

lead to the general acquisition of such values, and bring about the desired change that India needs at this stage. The highest ideal of life that emerged in Indian civilisation from Vedic times and embraces various aspects of Indian culture, education, and social order is best summarised as, *'Vasudhaiva Kutumbakam'* (the world is one family), and *'lokah samastah sukhino bhavantuh'* (let all be happy)!

The quest for knowledge and exploration of nature not only requires a comprehensive system of acquiring knowledge, but also the assurance that the tradition continues through a well-thought-out process of the transfer of knowledge to the generations to come. The traditional education system had led to the establishments of the *Gurukula*. The essence of highest thought and knowledge had to reach every home, hearth, and individual in society. Thus, *Dharma*, a way of life was dexterously absorbed and put to practice by one and all. The aims, objectives and pedagogical ideals of *Vidya* (knowledge), and *Avidya* (ignorance), as enunciated in the Vedic period, have eternal relevance. Indian society accorded the greatest respect and the highest place for the learned and the scholarly. Even kings and emperors took pride in extending the highest respect to *saints* and sages, to the *Acharya* (teacher) and *Kulapati* (head) of the *Gurukula* (the educational institute, the school)! These centres of learning were under no external influence, or interference, not even from the king or the State. The obligation on the part of society and the State was to ensure that no learning centre suffered because of the inadequacy of resources. The responsibility of the *Gurukula* and other centres of education and learning was to prepare human beings imbued with ethics and values, with skills and learning that would help launch them in life and in an activity of their choice. Education was holistic in nature; it aimed at 'man-making' and acquiring professional skills, the critical requirement of 'life and living'.

The distinctive feature of Indian culture focuses on and emphasises the 'within nature' of man. Its significance lies in the global admiration for Indian culture and its supremacy in understanding spirituality and making it a part of everyday life. It always emphasised on the human being as an 'individual', as a unit within or integral to the universal unit, as contrasted to Greek culture that specialised on the status of man in society. It is the Indian concept of man that brings out the distinction sharply. In the words of Dr Sarvepalli Radhakrishnan:

> The ideal man of India is not the magnanimous man of Greece or the valiant knight of medieval Europe, but the free man of spirit, who has attained insight into the universal source by rigid discipline and practice of disinterested virtues, who has freed himself from the prejudices of his time and place. It is India's pride that it has clung fast to this ideal and produced in every generation and in every part of the country, from the time of the rise of the Upanishads and Buddha to Ramakrishna and Gandhi, men who strove successfully to realise this ideal.

What attracts global attention to Indian culture and philosophy could also be visualised in the strength of the comprehension of the concept of man as already articulated. This concentration with which ancient thinkers and seers got absorbed in 'looking within' did not distract them from envisioning the physical universe in its totality. Their contributions in mathematics, algebra, astronomy, cosmology, health, and all such aspects that were essential for the welfare of the people, excelled and were a part of the urge to explore. These attainments have, unfortunately, or deliberately, remained ignored over centuries devoted to the growth and development of science and technology in the West. Now, these are getting attention, arguably more from the West than from within India! Let a renewed era begin in the projected teacher orientation programmes that will help to acquaint them with the contemporary relevance of the Indian tradition of the quest for knowledge and culture.

The *rishis* and *munis*, saints and sages, discovered in-depth knowledge, put it into words, and disseminated it for human welfare, for the well-being of all. The *Shanti Mantra*, a prayer for universal well-being and peace says just that:

Om, sarve bhavantu sukhinaha
Sarve santu niramayah
Sarve bhadrani pashyantu
Ma kashchit duhkha bhagbhavet
Om Shanti, Shanti, Shanti

May all be prosperous and happy
May all be free of illness
May all see what is spiritually uplifting
May no one suffer
Om, Peace, Peace, Peace

Swami Vivekananda's Vision for Education

In this era, we are witnessing a weakening of the sincere, committed, and selfless pursuit of new knowledge. We certainly need a correction of the course. Who else can guide us better in this endeavour than Swami Vivekananda?

Almost 125 years ago, Swami Vivekananda said,
Education which does not help the common mass of people to equip themselves for the struggle for life, which does not bring out strength and character, a spirit of philanthropy, and the courage of a lion — is it worth the name? Real education is that which enables one to stand on one's own legs.

The current education system in India is weak on this front. It needs new insights and ideas. Every effort undertaken to reform the education sector—whether on education policy, programmes, implementation strategies or articulation of outcomes—can derive immense benefit from Swami Vivekananda's vision and philosophy.

Rabindranath Tagore once told French writer Romain Rolland: 'If you want to know India, study Vivekananda. In him, everything is positive and nothing negative.' Even today, if we wish to understand the Indian tradition of the quest for knowledge, the systems of creating, generating, disseminating, and utilising knowledge, there is no better resource and support than reading what Swami Vivekananda has said about education, its goals, objectives, relationship to the growth of civilisations, human advancement, and the welfare of the people.

Swami Vivekananda articulated with very deep understanding the rise and fall of India, the subjugation of its history, culture, and heritage. This degradation was the result of planned efforts to destabilise India's time-tested traditional yet dynamic education system. Swamiji himself was active in a period characterised by rampant poverty, hunger, demoralisation of a slave nation, and people resigned to their fate.

The British had successfully achieved an attitudinal transformation among the English-educated Indian elite who were overawed by the superiority of the West in every aspect—from knowledge, to culture, to social systems! When Swami Vivekananda appeared on the scene, people were hesitant to even talk of independence. After the unprecedented Uprising of 1857, the people had slid into a mode of subjugated acceptance yet again. The country needed someone to give a wake-up call; it was time again for the people to realise who they were, what they were missing, how they were deprived not only of their material affluence but also of their dignity, self-respect, and the sense of pride in their culture and heritage. Most importantly, they needed to know how their minds had been lured away from their own people—the same people who were reduced to living in inhuman conditions, people who had lost the will to resist injustice and humiliation. If resurgence was ever conceivable, it needed a *messiah* who knew India and Indians!

And knowing India was no easy task in view of the vast diversity in people and material, spiritual and religious pursuits, and systems of governance and delivering justice. Swamiji travelled the length and breadth of the nation, covering every nook and cranny, and what he saw, despite the abject poverty and inhuman state of living, convinced him of the inherent unity of the Indian nation and its people. He also realised how India could play a leading role on the global stage in an effort to create a world of social cohesion and human dignity. An earlier but very well-known example of comprehending and connecting India is that of Adi Shankaracharya in the eighth century. He realised the need to travel around and connect with the people, and in his short life, he established shrines that strengthened the unity of the people and also of the regions and places. In more recent times, we can also recall another example, of how Gopal Krishna Gokhale advised Mohandas Karamchand Gandhi to 'know India' before beginning his work in India after the name and fame he earned in South Africa. He, dutifully, travelled to every corner of the country and developed an understanding that could not be matched by any of his political associates, during the freedom struggle.

Swami Vivekananda declared: 'Education is manifestation of the perfection already in man!' He was quick to realise the cause of the decline of a great number of people who claimed to be the 'children of immortality, *Amritasya Putrah*!' They had already understood that 'All this that is changeful in this ephemeral world must be enveloped by the Lord'! The query, in spite of all this and much more about national degradation, was answered by Swamiji. The attitude to false superiority played the most prominent role in the downfall of the 'children of god'. While on the one hand, India boasted of Taxila, attracting learners from over sixty nations, its social structure gradually declined, and even a journey on the seas was declared sinful and invited heavy penalties.

How can any system, social structure or a civilisation, maintain its dynamism if it isolates itself from the world outside? In 1894, Swami Vivekananda said:

> To my mind, the one great cause of the downfall and the degeneration coming was the building of a wall of custom—whose foundation was hatred of others—round the nation, and the real aim of which in ancient times was to prevent the Hindu from coming in contact with the surrounding Buddhist nations. (*Complete Works of Swami Vivekananda, Vol. 4*)

In the same refrain, he offered the solution:
> Give and take is the law; and if India wants to raise herself once more, it is absolutely necessary that she brings out her treasures and throws them broadcast among the nations of the earth, and in return be ready to receive what others have to give her. Expansion is life, contraction is death. Love is life, and hatred is death. We commenced to die the day we began to hate other races; and nothing can prevent our death unless we come back to expansion, which is life.

Finally, he exhorted: 'We must mix with all the races of the Earth.' He elaborated very clearly:
> We want that education by which character is formed, strength of mind is increased, the intellect is expanded and by which one can stand on one's own feet....The end of all education, all training, should be man-making. The end and aim of all training are to make the man grow. The training, by which the current and expression of will are brought under control and become fruitful, is called education.

Character building and development of the personality are the two pivots on which the entire process of teaching and learning must evolve. The traditional Indian education system judged the individual not by the riches accumulated but the knowledge acquired and the values practised in life.

Swami Vivekananda had already clarified that, 'It is man-making education all round that we want'. He further emphasised that the end of all education has to be man-making just as the end of all training is to make the man grow. He also said:

> Education is not the amount of information that is put into your brain and runs riot there, undigested, all your life. We must have life-building, man-making, character-making assimilation of ideas. If you have assimilated five ideas and made them your life and character, you have more education than any man who has got by heart a whole library.

The lamp that was lit by Swami Vivekananda spread its radiance across the nation, across communities and the entire world now realises and relishes India's global presence. But mere world-wide travel and opening up the seashores and airports is only one initial step. It alone is not sufficient to give Indians their due on the global stage. If India wants to stand with her head high in the global community, she has to prepare its younger generations, such young people who are self-assured, confident, and proud of their heritage, history, and motherland, and are keen to prove that they are not inferior to anyone. They must believe in their capability and potential to lead a global renaissance.

For a committed researcher and explorer, the pursuit of knowledge is a pious task. Indian culture and tradition must connect with our urge to gain better understanding of the forces of nature and utilise that knowledge for the welfare of the people, humanity and that, too, without any distinction or selfish motive. Every soul is divine. And the one who recognises this, prays for one and all—men and women of all religions and faiths, of all colours and creeds, with no distinction.

Teachers of today and tomorrow would do well if they recall the wisdom of Socrates: 'I cannot teach anybody, I can only make them think.' Sri Aurobindo had said it in very simple but meaningful terms: 'Nothing can be taught' and that 'mind must be consulted in its own growth'. Once these simple-looking elements are properly internalised by the teachers, it would not be tough for them to visualise their changed role.

Mahatma Gandhi on Education in India

Mohandas Karamchand Gandhi had very strong and definite views on the system of education in India. He envisioned in 1922:

> But there is hope, if education spreads throughout the country. From that people would develop from their childhood qualities of pure conduct, god-fearing, and love. Swaraj would give us happiness only when we attain success in the task. Otherwise, India becomes the abode for grave injustice and tyranny of the rulers.

How prophetic were his words! Should Indian education system not get deep into ascertaining what has gone wrong within, and outside, the system of education?

He further asserted:

Pupils should know to discriminate between what should be received and what rejected. It is the duty of the teacher to teach his pupils discrimination. If we go on talking indiscriminately, we would be no better than machines. We are thinking, knowing beings and must in this period distinguish truth from untruth. Sweet from the bitter language, clean from the unclean, and so on.

Coming from a visionary blessed with unparalleled foresight, this could be considered a statement of expectations from the education of the future!

Children would be extremely pleased to learn of

Gandhiji's views on textbooks:
> I do not want children to have any textbooks. The teacher may, if they so wish, read them. We may write as much for them as we please. If you write for children, you may make the teachers mechanical and destroy their originality and initiative. I do not, of course, wish to arrest the progress of teachers.... Where the people need their books, by all means buy them, but please understand what lies behind my attitude.

He devoted time and energy to envision the shape of education in the post-independence period in India. He wanted craft, art, health, and education to be integrated into the process of teaching and learning. *Nai Talim* (new education or learning) to him, was a beautiful blend of all the four. He found it consistent with the environment in India which is (and it definitely was during his time), predominantly rural. Education, he said:,

> Believes in establishing equilibrium between the body, the mind, and the spirit of which man is made. It is unlike the Western type, which is predominantly militarist, in which the mind and the body are the primary care of education to the subordination of the spirit. This is best done when education is given through handicraft.

He could propose this because of his deep understanding of the Indian mind, needs and aspirations on the one hand, and experiences gained through his personal experiments in education in his ashrams on the other.

His historic speech at the Royal Institute of International

Affairs at Chatham House, London, on 20 October 1931, articulated the decline of Indian education after the arrival of the British:

> I say without fear of my figures being challenged successfully, that today India is more illiterate than it was fifty or a hundred years ago, and so is Burma, because the British administrators, when they came to India, instead of taking hold of things as they were, began to root them out. They scratched the soil and began to look at the root, and left the root like that, and the beautiful tree perished.

Sir Philip Hartog challenged Gandhiji, who remained steadfast in his conviction. Subsequently, eminent thinker and researcher, Dharampal, established the fact based on documentary evidence extracted from the records created by the British officers that Gandhiji was absolutely correct. The most important strategic intervention in sustaining the British hold over India was through education that was to destroy the age-old edifice of knowledge creation, transfer to generations ahead and its application in the welfare not only of the individual but of the people. In the process, they succeeded in 'delinking Indians from their history, culture and heritage'. They attacked the roots of that beautiful tree, and it dried up.

The British policy succeeded beyond expectations for the alien rulers, as Indians grabbed the bait of Western knowledge, culture, language, and its 'superiority'. It has not yet been erased. Let the implementers remember the defects Gandhi had identified in a long article in the *Young India* issue of 1 August 1921, just a little over a hundred

years ago! Declaring the then system as faulty, apart from its association with an utterly unjust government, he pointed out three defects in the then prevailing education system:
1. Based on foreign culture to the almost entire exclusion of indigenous culture
2. Ignores the culture of the heart and the hand, and confines itself simply to the head
3. Real education is impossible through a foreign medium

In the *Young India* of 1 June 1921, he wrote:
> I do not want my house to be walled in all sides and my windows to be stuffed. I want the cultures of all the lands to be blown about my house as freely as possible. But I refuse to be blown off my feet by any. I refuse to live in other people's houses as an interloper, a beggar or a slave.

Although Gandhiji had warned about all this in *Hind Swaraj, written* in 1909, India remained overly enamoured of all that was Western, and we remained overwhelmed, and overeager to borrow everything from 'there and them'.

Gandhiji expressed in *Young India* of 1 September 1921:
> It is my firm opinion that no culture has treasures so rich as ours. We have not known it; we have been made even to depreciate its value. We have almost ceased to live it.

Let us hope that the proposed educational reforms would prepare young persons with credentials, and that they would be looking after the masses. Education must lead to human dignity, tone, and more. He always emphasised the need to relate with the roots and the need for being fit for that was the need of the nation.

He further articulated these thoughts in the same issue of *Young India*:

Whatever may be true of other countries, in India at any rate where more than eighty percent of the population is agricultural and another ten percent industrial, it is a crime to make education merely literacy, and to unfit boys and girls for manual work in after-life. Indeed, I hold that as the larger part of our time is devoted to labour for earning our bread, our children must from their infancy be taught the dignity of such labour. Our children should not be so taught as to despise having gone to school should become useless, as he does become, as an agricultural labourer. It is a sad thing that our schoolboys look upon manual labour with disfavour, if not contempt.

He consistently talked of the India of his dreams, and this included his concerns about the impediments ahead. These were evident in the seven social sins he talked about in the *Young India* issue of 22 October 1925:
- politics without principles
- wealth without work
- pleasure without conscience
- knowledge without character
- commerce without morality
- science without humanity
- worship without sacrifice

No policy, education policy included, could ignore the severity of these sins in the present times. One could, in the present context, have a relook at these and reformulate them, but it would be perilous to neglect any. The 'sins' are taking stronger roots, the 'tensions' are disturbing human habitation and systems are already under severe strain and pressure. These are the consequences of declining moral, ethical, and humanistic considerations. Education is the only ray of hope to achieve the much required attitudinal transformation among the generations ahead.

In his 1932 book, *Remakers of Mankind,* Carl Washburne writes that when Mahatma Gandhi was asked what his goal in education was, when India obtained self-rule, Gandhi answered that it was 'Character-building'. He said: 'I would try to develop courage, strength, virtue, the ability to forget oneself in working towards great aims. This is more important than literacy; academic learning is only a means to this great end.'

Character formation was the strength of the traditional Indian system of knowledge quest that included creation, generation, utilisation, and transfer of knowledge to generations ahead. With all the experiences gained globally in varying contexts and approaches, it is now accepted globally that education in every country must be rooted in its culture and committed to progress. Character-building just cannot be envisioned in isolation to culture. No culture can flourish in isolation and every effort must be made to make children well-aware and conversant with their own culture before being introduced to other cultures. India painfully suffered as the transplanted system that deliberately kept young 'educated' Indians debarred from getting familiar with the nuances of their own culture, while they were systematically indoctrinated in the superiority of western culture.

Gandhiji wrote in the weekly newspaper, *Harijan,* on March 8, 1935:

> In my opinion, intelligent labour is for the time being the only primary and adult education in this land of starving millions. Literacy education should follow

the education of the hand—the one gift that visibly distinguishes man from beast. It is a superstition to think that the fullest development of man is impossible without a knowledge of the art of reading and writing. That knowledge undoubtedly adds grace to life, but it is in no way indispensable for man's moral, physical, or material growth.

Later in the *Harijan* of 8 May 1937, he wrote:
Man is neither mere intellect, nor the gross animal body, nor the heart nor Soul alone. A proper and harmonious combination of all the three is required for the whole man and constitutes the true economics of education.

Based upon his experiences and experiments in education, Mohandas Karamchand Gandhi finally proposed the idea of *Buniyadi Talim*, basic education, in the Wardha Conference in 1937.

The concept was the outcome of Gandhiji's experience with colonialism and the English educational system. He could perceive that Indian children would be alienated from their traditions and culture, and that they would be directed to 'career-based thinking'. The negative outcomes he warned against were the disdain for manual labour, the development of a new elite class, and the increasing problems of urbanisation and industrialisation.

The three pillars of Gandhiji's pedagogy were focusing on the lifelong character of education, its social character and its holistic process. Education had to mean 'moral development', a lifelong process. The emphasis should be on *Buniyadi Talim*—on transforming the learner into a complete personality, a person of strong character.

Reiterating the words of Swami Vivekananda, what we need, is 'man-making education', Gandhi said that by education, he 'an all-round drawing out of the best in child and man—body, mind and spirit'.

The future requires us to develop an attitude to accept 'lifelong learning' as part of life by young and old alike. It demands a high level of professional commitment, dynamism and vision on the part of policy makers and implementers with inputs from academicians and scholars. We have the issues of accepting diversity, achieving social cohesion and religious amity as the necessary ingredients in making life better for all. Nelson Mandela once said:

> The power of education extends beyond the development of skills we need for economic success. It can contribute to nation-building and reconciliation.

The seeds of growth, development and progress are sown in primary schools where value inculcation and nurturance must begin in right earnest by suitably abled teachers working in an environment that is conducive to learning and encourages interaction.

Through *Buniyadi Talim,* Gandhi wanted every child to, 'acquire the capacity for self-reliance in every aspect of a clean, healthy and cultured life, together with an understanding of social and moral implications of such a life'. If this aspect had found adequate place and importance in the scheme of things in Indian education, we would not have been burdened with Vice-Chancellors with fake degrees or those enhancing marks of engineering graduates without considering the social and moral implications of their misdeeds.

Working with their hands was considered essential as

in Indian conditions, it would ensure a reasonable level of earning for everyone. India could have reaped rich dividends if this aspect was given its due not only in policy formulations but also at the implementation stage. Education, however, is also the process of 'manifesting the perfection already in man'. This concept of perfection includes preparing the person for addressing various problems that human beings encounter in society.

The 'Sarvodya' that Gandhiji learnt while in South Africa, after reading John Ruskin's book *Unto this Last*: stated:

- The good of the individual is contained in the good of all.
- A lawyer's work has the same value as the barber's, in as much as all have the same right of earning their livelihood from their work.
- That the life of a labour, that is, the tiller of the soil and the handicraftsman, is the life worth living.

Rabindranath Tagore's Vision of Education

On 22 December 1901, history was created in the annals of Indian education when Rabindranath Tagore inaugurated his school in Shantiniketan. Various aspects of education and learning were churning in his mind all along ever since he, as a child, experienced what all goes on in schools. Gradually, he evolved his own perception of the process of knowledge acquisition and began the planning for giving it a practical shape. He began by teaching his own children but found out that sporadic initiatives would not do. Krishna Kripalani puts it in these words: 'Having suffered from bad teaching in his childhood, he had thought much, and written also, on the fundamentals of teaching and now he gained a new insight by putting his principles into practice. But teaching one's children haphazardly is not enough, he needed a wider field for systematic experimentation and he thought, why not shift to Shantiniketan and start a small experimental school there? His thought process was already influenced by the ancient *Gurukula* system and the way knowledge was dispensed and acquired there in a natural way! The sages and saints lived with their pupils, presented the ideal of simple living and high, rather, universal thinking! Tagore was convinced that the best teacher was nature. He wanted to recreate the joyful, soulful, and inspiring environment of the *Tapovan*s that could add grace and beauty to the entire process of learning, internalising knowledge and acquiring skills to utilise it for the welfare of the people. Revival and inclusion of the basics of the ancient Indian system was the only way out of the soulless and mechanical system that had replaced it.

Rabindranath Tagore summarised the essence of his educational ideas when he declared that the great use of education was, 'To know man and to make oneself known to man!' And towards this, everyone must get a chance to learn the language of the intellect and also the 'language of Art' that is essential for total personality development. His own experiences of schooling were indeed highly uninspiring and depressing and were based on thoughts such as hard benches, dull prison-like walls, and the 'Master' who possibly seemed evil! Whenever he entered the classroom, the benches and the tables, he said, 'elbowing and jostling their way in to my mind, appeared... stiff, cramping, and dead'. The overall environment in most of the schools remains more or less as unattractive and uninviting as in the times of Rabindranath's childhood. It is still the same painful, over-stressing, and creativity-killing environment that maintains the regime of 'cram and exam'. Even at home, learning became a 'task' that must be performed mechanically. 'As I read I nod, then jerk myself again with a start but miss far more than I read. When finally, I tumble into bed I have at least a little time to call my own,' he said. His unpleasant experiences both in school and private teaching at home convinced him this was not the system that encouraged the flowering of human talent and personality. Whatever time he spent in schooling and initial learning gave him the, 'Knowledge of the wrong from which children of men suffer.' The so-called discipline in the school practically debarred students from participating in activities that naturally attracted them, and they felt fettered and imprisoned. He could never reconcile to the idea of children made to sit like, in what he describes as 'Specimen of some museum in classrooms, while lessons are being pelted at them from high like hailstorm on flowers.'

All that he experienced, and disliked, fired the imagination of young Rabindranath to visualise better ways of imparting education to students! And this thought process that began rather early resulted in the creation of the persona of the Gurudev! His search for a universal humane approach to the existing system of imparting and receiving education, knowledge and wisdom was a lifelong process. As the scion of a Zamindar family, with a very sensitive and humane mind, his lifelong passion was not only education, culture, and art, but also the economic rehabilitation of the Indian villager. His consistent and lifelong interest was the welfare of Indian peasants. Simultaneously, the sensitive poet was keenly observing the people of India, their misery and strengths, selfishness and readiness to sacrifice, patience and heroism, sense of resignation to fate and in the process, accepting injustice without manly retaliation. He understood India, its people, its tradition of the knowledge quest, its contemporary relevance and the deficiencies that grew because of lack of dynamism and reluctance to keep pace with current times. While his outstanding contributions in the intellectual arena are recognised and revered throughout India, and abroad, his singular and sensitivity-filled initiatives for the masses are often overshadowed by it. Not many know that he had, along with Shantiniketan, also founded a parallel institution—Shri Niketan for the welfare of the peasants who create the cornerstone of the Indian economy. They needed support including new ideas and skills, outputs of new experiments and innovations that were possible and feasible because of the developments in science and technology. He donated part of the Nobel Prize amount to his school in Shantiniketan and invested a substantial portion in a cooperative bank, created to help needy peasants on his family estate.

He realised that people need to be inspired, told about their inner potential and how to manifest it, how to move out of the shackles of despondency and rejuvenate their lives through the regeneration of self-assurance, and acquisition of the requisite levels of knowledge and skills. It was his sensitivity to the lives of the common-man-around that a considerable number of his stories were woven around their lives, times, and travails. He was convinced that the objective of education was to bring about excellence in human lives by the light of education that was known to dispel the darkness of ignorance. His idea of education did not mean pedantic acquisition of knowledge but true wisdom: 'We have to keep in mind the fact that love and action are the only mediums through which perfect knowledge can be obtained, for the object of knowledge is not pedantry but wisdom.' Once the individual expands his canvas through awareness and education, he can express himself with self-assurance, and that fills him with a sense of complete freedom that every one wishes to achieve: 'Apathy and ignorance are the worst forms of bondage for man; they are the invisible walls of confinement that we carry around us when we are in their grip,' he believed.

Once the clouds of darkness are dispersed through the light of the right education, given and received in a congenial and sensitive environment, it would be easy to comprehend the 'Unity of Truth'! This is one aspect that is creating so much of turmoil in human existence at this stage. It manifests in the shape of wars, violence, distrust, fundamentalism, insecurity, misery, hunger, and poverty. To move ahead to ameliorate inhuman trends and tendencies, education systems should not only focus on the intellectual aspect but equally on the physical, intellectual, and emotional aspect. The need for this is, in some way, being acknowledged and accepted in terms of the 'Spiritual Quotient'. It requires serious consideration by policy makers of current times, As Rabindranath Tagore said in a lecture that he delivered in America:

> The young mind should be saturated with the idea that it has been born in a human world, which is in harmony with the world around it. And this is what your regular type of school ignores with an air of superior wisdom, severe and disdainful. It forcibly snatches children away from a world full of mystery of God's own handiwork full of the suggestiveness of personality.

It is evident that he would like every learner to be well

aware of his responsibility to strengthen the sensitive bond between man and nature. And that would be possible and practical only when human beings learn to respect each other, realise the unity in diversity, and appreciate the beauty of diversity of every conceivable variety, including religious diversity.

Familiarity with the basics of Tagore's philosophy of education could go a long way in reorienting the present system that is causing much concern to practically every thinking mind. The inadequacies of personality development, internalisation of the values of social cohesion and religious amity, human responsibility in maintaining sensitive man-nature relationship are now appearing before us in frightening proportions. The system Tagore envisioned is universally applicable. It could also be interpreted as a total acceptance of *Vasudhaiva Kutumbakam* in pragmatic terms. It is time India reconsiders the basics of its education policy and systemic structures on this one count: is it nurturing the power of ideas and imagination, among learners, or is it stunting them? It's time to encourage and inspire curiosity and creativity to flourish without any shackles. It has organic link to the process of growth and development of India and the Indian people.

Rabindranath Tagore mentioned in yet another one of his lectures that, 'It was often alleged that Asia would never progress ahead as it has turned its face backward.' It has been proven wrong by countries like Japan, China, and India. Equally, South Asia and Southeast Asian regions have proven it wrong. All these countries have moved ahead, without either ignoring the past, or ignoring new knowledge. People here are not perpetually lost in the sweet slumber of the glory of the past, oblivious to the need to move ahead in times, and keep pace with it! Probably realising this, Mahatma Gandhi indicated he would open the windows and doors of his house for the fresh air of ideas and knowledge, but not permit the opening to be so wide as to blow out one's own house! It is one thing to be proud of one's history, culture, tradition of knowledge growth, scriptures, and literature, but it is also necessary to examine whether that alone is sufficient for all times ahead.

Focus on Indigenous Education

It is interesting to note that education was given the highest priority by the leaders of the Indian freedom struggle. This was indeed unique as its importance was realised both in political forums and also among philosophers and intellectuals. Several of them presented a philosophy of education that could have helped develop a model of education that was 'rooted to culture and committed to progress'! The moral and ethical angle was never ignored or neglected in these formulations. At the time of Independence, India had a strong indigenous philosophical base established over the decades by Swami Vivekananda, Swami Dayananda, Mahatma Gandhi, Sri Aurobindo, and Rabindranath Tagore. They knew India, its people and practices, tradition and culture. Above all, India's tradition of knowledge quest has fetched global admiration for India's rise in spirituality.

In their vision of Independent India, the leaders of the time were very clear on the priorities. There was persistent focus on indigenous universal education in free India. The leaders knew that the transplanted system forced by foreign rulers was not suitable in free India. It was meant for a few, with a specific objective, and would crash if extended on a universal scale. Sadly enough, India continued with it. Could one say that we preferred continuity and status-quo instead of creating, 'Our schools, our campuses, our programmes, our curricula, our libraries and laboratories as the vision outlined by Dadabhai Naoroji in his plea for elementary education for all children?

In 1911 Gopal Krishna Gokhale moved a Bill and a resolution in the Central Legislature (1910-1912) to this effect. It was, as expected, rejected. Implementation of this century-old aspiration could become a legal realty only in 2010. Who does not recall the emphasis that Mahatma Gandhi laid on education for all? In 2010, the recommendation on Continuous and Comprehensive Evaluation (CCE) too was presented as if it was a great innovative and historic recommendation being made for the first time! Unfortunately, it was not so. The Kothari Commission (1964-66) had made comprehensive recommendations on examination reforms. J P Naik, illustrious educationist and secretary of the Kothari Commission had summarised the recommendations on examination reforms in his book, *Education Commission and After*, published in 1979. He had incisively scrutinised the implementation of the commission report and the National Policy on Education of 1968. He wrote:

- The Commission suggested that we should move in the direction of abolishing external examinations and replacing them by a system of continuous internal evaluation (para 11.53).
- Remuneration to examiners (the vested interest that tends to perpetuate the system) should be abolished (para 11.57).
- More frequent periodical assessments should be

introduced to reduce the importance of final and external tests and the examination technique improved (paras 11.54 and 11.55).
- The certificate at the end-of-school examinations should simply state the performance of the candidate without any declaration of having passed or failed (para 9.80).
- A system of complete internal assessment of students, which is not mixed with external examination results, be developed (para 9.84).

These recommendations were of far-reaching consequences and had the potential to give the impetus to the education system moving ahead in practically all of its aspects.

Let us scrutinise the strength of another recommendation:
- Examinations, especially public examinations, should be made more objective and reliable.
- Evaluation should enable the teacher to see the effectiveness of his instruction and enable the pupils to judge the results of their learning efforts.
- It should thus act as an instrument of improving both the teaching and learning processes including the content of courses and method of teaching (15.1).

Obviously, these recommendations included acceptance of the CCE. J P Naik lamented that 'Very little practical effect has been given to these recommendations' and that in spite of well-established unreliability of external examinations, we continue to depend rather solely on them! Over the years, conditions have become more and more unfavourable for implementing the CCE. Teacher shortage, teacher absenteeism, inadequate infrastructure support and an uninviting environment in schools, lethargic approach to regular teacher recruitment and general deterioration could be cited as the obvious contributors. It was necessary in 2010 to have analysed the existing scenario before announcing a three-year time frame of no exams and the introduction of CCE. Non-comprehension of ground level reality in 2010, once again, delayed the universalisation of education by at least another decade.

The growth of unbiased and the pure professional tradition of the quest for knowledge suffers in conditions of severe apathy towards the indigenous tradition of knowledge creation and dissemination, the essence of which may still be relevant. It is now globally acknowledged that education in every country must be rooted to culture and committed to progress. The pre-Independence model of Gandhi and Zakir Husain was based upon this premise. It is now being realised if India had given it the importance it deserved, things would have been far more encouraging on the employment front, as also there would have been no exodus from rural areas. Education has suffered because of the lack of courage to link it to the national tradition of growth of knowledge and scholarship instead of overdependence on an inherited legacy.

It should never be tough for a professional, unbiased educationist to conclude that education in every country must be a product of the indigenous thought process and appropriate new scientific knowledge. Consequently, the first requirement at the policy planning level is full familiarity with indigenous traditions of the knowledge quest, its creation, generation, transfer, and utilisation. This is necessary, but not a closed exercise. It would be equally necessary to acquire a deep comprehension of new knowledge that could be available from all possible sources and places.

Upheaval at the Advent of the 20th Century

The twentieth century witnessed the end of the colonial era, and the initiation of the subsequent transition into another era of progress and development among the newly-liberated nations. Most of these nations were deficient in human resources at every level: education, experience, and expertise. Most of them had transplanted their education systems established over the ruins of indigenous traditions of the knowledge quest. The shortage of educated and skilled manpower emerged as a great impeder in evolving the indigenous ideology of progress and development by internal experts. In most of the cases, the ideology of progress and growth was borrowed from the West, and implemented under active guidance of the former rulers.

Another contributing factor was the fascination of all that was foreign, western, and modern! Exploitative, ethically weak, and unprofessionally envisioned plans and programmes of development led to a serious imbalance in social, economic, and man-nature relationships. In India, Gandhi, Gram Swaraj, the farmer, the village, and local partisan and production skills, were all ignored, leading to serious neglect of the agriculture sector.

The devastation of WWII, and the growing public opinion against wars and violence highlighted the need for international cooperation and collaboration among nations. It led to the creation of the United Nations (UN), the United Nations Educational, Scientific and Cultural Organization, (UNESCO), the UNICEF (United Nations International Childrens' Educational Fund, the World

Health Organization (WHO), the United Nations Security Council (UNSC), and several other organisations. There had to be a partnership among all nations on equal and dignified terms. That was the only way to tackle global issues and concerns.

Basic Elements of Interfaith Education

Children must learn how human existence is viewed and visualised in different religions. After all, as they grow up, they have to live in a multicultural and multi-religious society. Their process of growing up would be deficient if they did not know the basics of religions, other than their own. Now that the infamous Aryan Invasion Theory stands busted scientifically, there should be no hesitation in acknowledging that the ancient Indian culture and religion were civilised and advanced enough to attract people of different ethnicity, linguistic backgrounds, and faiths, who arrived at the shores of India. Hugh Murray's *Historical Account of Discoveries and Travels in Asia* (Vol. 2, p. 20), gives the impressions of Abdul Razak about what he saw in the State of Calicut:

> The People (of Calicut) are infidels, consequently, I consider myself in an enemy country, as the Mohammedans consider anyone who has not received the Koran. Yet, I admit that I met with perfect toleration, and even favour, we have two mosques and are allowed to pray in public.

Abdul Razak effectively reveals how the concept of 'infidel', which he had learnt earlier, was in direct contrast to the 'acceptance of otherness' that he experienced in India. It is this aspect that could create a harmonious and peaceful society in our present-day world.

The core elements of ancient Indian civilisation are so clearly articulated by His Holiness the Dalai Lama:

> Sometimes I describe myself as a modern-day messenger of ancient Indian thought. Two of the most important ideas I share wherever I travel are—the principle of nonviolence and interreligious harmony. Both are drawn from ancient Indian heritage. Though I am of course a Tibetan, I also consider myself to be, in a sense, a son of India. Since childhood my mind has been nourished by the classics of Indian thought.... So, I am very happy to share and promote this Indian understanding of secularism, as I believe it can be of great value to all humanity.

The rich tradition of the acceptance of the other that we have as our ancient heritage, bestows us with the singular responsibility to guide nations that are experiencing the influx of people from other countries with differing world views, faiths, languages, ethnicity and culture, and in significant proportions. We, in India, can do it only when our own house is in order and people from outside appreciate it as a practical reality.

In the globalised and interconnected world, conflicts of alarming proportions can develop in the future if not seriously countered by all concerned. Our responsibility increases manifold when the global expectation is expressed in the words of Arnold Toynbee, '...At this supremely dangerous moment in human history, the only way of salvation for mankind is the Indian way.' To those who may ask 'why?' Dr Toynbee has the answer, 'Here we have an attitude and spirit that can make it possible for the human race to grow together in to a single family, and in the Atomic age, this is the only alternative to destroying ourselves.' The only possible strategy is to nourish and educate the generations ahead on the universality of ancient Indian thought and practice. Education is the key to create a global family that accepts equality of all faiths and religions. All religions are equally true, all have the same goal, and all are striving to reach it following different paths. The gravity of the growing challenge before humanity is enormous. Inclusive growth and progress are unfathomable in a world without peace and harmony.

A major aspect of this challenge is those elements that still believe that their religion, language, tradition, practices, and culture alone are superior to those of others, taken together or separately, and, hence, their task is to bring everyone under a single umbrella, in any which way! The major chunk of violence, terrorism, and insecurity inflicted on mankind arises out of ill-conceived fanaticism and fundamentalism. The elements that inspire and encourage ignorant, impressionable, and vulnerable persons to erase the presence of other religions deserve no place in the global society of the twenty-first century. The silent and suffering majority must now become vocal and assertive.

Every step must be taken to ensure that children and young people are saved from all machinations and mal-intentions. The only way is to re-look at the systems of education, formal, social, cultural, and informal. The essence of futuristic education systems that could lead to a world of peace and cohesion would be woven around respect for life in all it different forms, and acceptance of the other.

Human beings are blessed with the gift of the power of ideas and imagination. They love their freedom. Their thinking power, analytical capacity, and creative skills need nurturance and guidance. In the absence of such learning, great harm is perpetrated by fundamentalism and intolerance. And this is all done in the name of the Almighty, the Ultimate Truth, and hopes of a smooth transition to Heaven. The uncouth, ignorant, and uncivilised who succeed in their nefarious designs are usually among those deprived of right education in their initial years.

For ages, efforts have been made by men of eminence and of wisdom and knowledge, to show the right path to all human beings, but the impact has, all along, been only partial. Education is, however, still the ray of hope. The world of today and tomorrow needs education that is imbued with interfaith values that nurtures respect for otherness. Eminent interfaith scholar, Maulana Wahiduddin Khan puts this in simple terms:

> The Truth is that for the attainment of disciplined behaviour, it is essential for one to be convinced of the existence of a power far superior to himself, a Being who is aware of man's activities at every moment, who can reward and punish man, and from whom it is impossible to escape.

Every religion acknowledges and accepts the presence of God who alone would fit in this expectation, and description. From this logic–some may disagree–could emerge the contours of the content and process of education.

Today's Perspective

The world, especially the West, as we know it can take the example of Ancient India that was known to live with harmony with people of different communities and religions and speaking a variety of dialects. People, all over the world, are now closely interacting because of globalisation, ease of mobility and in their desire to seek greener pastures, in search of security and livelihood. If India was still high on its record of social cohesion and religious amity, and on its adherence to the joint family systems and social security, and on basing its democracy on values defined by Gandhi and the spirit of the freedom struggle, these nations would have now flocked to India to learn more. Deeply satisfied, they would declare it as their *Guru*, without India itself making such a claim! If we were a learning hub, and had institutions like Nalanda, Taxila, Vikramshila and others, the *Gurukula* concept would have remained unchallenged. India needs to become a great global learning hub.

Swami Vivekananda presented India and its past glory to the world, and the values that it had adhered to in the past, highlighting the concerns it had shown towards the welfare of all without any discrimination at the World's Parliament of Religions in 1893. He received global acclaim and admiration. He knew that speaking of the concepts alone was not sufficient. He established the *Ramakrishna Missions* worldwide. Yes, we need institutions that prepare the youth and give them 'man-making' education. Let them comprehend that 'Education is the perfection already in man!' he had said.

Gurudev Tagore predicted that, 'India is destined to be the teacher of the world'. He did not travel the globe to declare that India would be a *Vishwa Guru* (world teacher). Instead, he established the institutions that had all the ingredients of a *Gurukula*, along with every feature of a modern-day international knowledge hub. Similarly, this aspect was elaborated by Sri Aurobindo. He predicted, 'India will be the moral leader of the world.' He established the Auroville Ashram in Pondicherry. These give an idea how international relationships could indeed be given a sound cultural knowledge, and spiritual base, to strengthen the moral basis of relationships. It was the continuity of this moral tradition that Gandhi referred to when he talked of, 'Commerce without morality' and 'Wealth without work' among the seven social sins that he first wrote about in 1925. Incidentally, he also included, 'Knowledge without character'. India needs to relearn, and create knowledge hubs of its own.

The Post-Independence Era

In the last seven decades, we have moved ahead only in bits and pieces in education quality reforms. Now that elementary education has been practically universalised, at least in enrolment and participation, we must focus on transforming every learner, from a person into a personality. This is in sync with the famous Gandhian articulation of 'bringing out the best out of body, mind and spirit' in all. Once all three of these flourish in the right environment and the interest of children is monitored, then we would be moving in the right direction on the path of vitality, self-assurance and confidence. Yes, teachers would have to accept what Sri Aurobindo had taught us that nothing can be taught, and that the mind must be consulted for its development. Once education puts the learner on the path of his own liking and special interest, it would be possible to expect — in the words of Swami Vivekananda:

> The whole gist of this teaching is that you should work like a master and not like a slave, work incessantly, but do not do slave's work.... work through freedom! Work

through love! That is what education must achieve: every learner internalises the values of Truth, Peace, Nonviolence, Righteous Conduct, and Love.

Onward Journey

When we got our Independence, we were free to evolve, implement, and develop our unique system of education, one rooted in culture and committed to progress! It must be acknowledged that Independent India paid scant attention to investment in education all along, although it did implement a constitutional provision that ensured free and compulsory education to all children, 'till they attain 14 years of age'. However, an epistemological base to create an indigenous system of education was not extricated.

India had a unique, fulsome, advanced and well-evolved comprehension of the real purpose of education that can be summed up in Swami Vivekananda's words when he outlined that 'Education is the manifestation of perfection already in man....' UNESCO, in the much talked of Delors Commission, accepts in the title of the Report, Learning the Treasure Within! How much India has traditionally valued knowledge is known to us for centuries in such a subtle statement: *Yavadjeevait adhiyate viprah* (The wise continue to gain knowledge throughout their lives). This now reverberates globally as Lifelong Learning. When Mahatma Gandhi said that he would like education to bring the best out of body, mind and spirit, he was emphasising the essence of the Indian approach to skill development, learning, acquisition of knowledge and scholarship, and personality development that prepares young people to dedicate themselves in the service of one and all. This ideology fits in perfectly well with the contemporary and global thinking on education, as indicated in the Delors Commission Report: 'In confronting many challenges that the future holds in store, humankind sees in education an indispensable asset in its attempts to attain the ideals of peace, freedom and social justice.' As it concludes its work, the Commission affirms its belief that education has a fundamental role to play in personal and social development. It does not see education as a miracle cure or a magic formula opening the door to a world in which all ideals will be attained, but as one of the principal means available to foster a deeper and more harmonious form of human development and thereby reduce poverty, exclusion, ignorance, oppression and war. Education generates hope, and spreads light in the darkness.

Chapter 2

Global Educational Scenario and Emerging Trends

Knowledge creation is a continuous process of combining, converting, and transferring different kinds of knowledge as is the skill of acquiring and refining knowledge. The capability to acquire, create, and utilise knowledge to enhance quality of life is what distinguishes human beings from other living beings on this planet. We learn from the *Bhagavad Gita* that there is nothing purer than *jnana* (knowledge). The world has, over the last one hundred years, transitioned from an information-based society to a knowledge-based one, and the advancement toward a wisdom society has begun. But is education only about acquiring knowledge or creating new knowledge? No, it is much more than that, and this must be closely searched and every new policy document on education critically reviewed.

To recall Bertrand Russell's essay Knowledge and Wisdom: Man has no chance of survival if knowledge only remains knowledge but if he could transform knowledge into wisdom, he would not only survive but would be able to ascend to greater and greater heights of achievements.

Yes, we need to prepare young persons who have an alert faculty of critical thinking, vibrant analytical skills, and awareness that knowledge is meaningless if is not utilised towards the welfare of the larger human community. Think of the Manhattan Project, the Trinity test south of Los Alamos on 16 July 1945. Knowledge was on a high, but while scientists were exploring the possible utilisation of Atomic and Nuclear energy in the best interest of humanity, in areas such as medicine, land use, clean energy, and so on, those in power and authority had other ideas, driven by the World War, and thus decided to drop the Atom bomb on Hiroshima and Nagasaki, in Japan, respectively on 6 and 9 August 1945. This was among the most cruel and shameful acts perpetrated in human history at that time! Much before the devastation of Hiroshima, Mahatma Gandhi had pointed to 'Knowledge without Character' as one of the seven social sins. Education has no meaning if it is not used as a vehicle for character building.

Education today must prepare us to 'learn to learn more', and imbibe the keenness for lifelong learning. We must get acquainted with ancient Indian culture, history, and heritage; there can be no let-up in acquiring knowledge. We need to however, selectively, keep the doors and windows open, respect knowledge from every source, and have respect for every culture, tradition, language, and ethnicity. Such is the world we all must strive to create. Education that relies on the five eternal values of truth, peace, nonviolence, dharma, and love, will play a great sobering role in preparing generations ahead. The youth of today should be equipped to become prominent contributors in creating a world of peace, a world that accepts and appreciates diversity and, at the same time, become a votary of universal unity.

Global Educational Change and the Indian Context

The sector of education has numerous challenges before it. Post-independence, while it could claim huge advances in terms of the increasing numbers of institutions and enrolments at each stage, it has still much to accomplish in terms of quality of the products, their suitability for the job market and also the level of entrepreneurial skills acquired before they begin their professional life. The most significant challenge can be comprehended in the query: is the Indian education system equipped enough to prepare its young persons to take advantage of the much-hyped 'demographic dividend' as the 'nation of the young'? Even in this arena, several other countries are also ready with their well-educated and skilled young persons, offering tough competition to Indian students. Within India, practically every sector of governance, from personnel in the security forces to teachers in schools, suffers from manpower deficiency in huge numbers, while millions of young persons have waited for decades to get jobs!

Sustainable Development

The core global concern is to trace the path of sustainable development. In 2015, the General Assembly of the United Nations recognised UNESCO as the lead Agency,

> To continue to provide coordination for the implementation of the Global Action Plan (GAP) on Education for Sustainable Development (ESD) in cooperation with partners, advocate for adequate resources for ESD, support member-states in building capacity, promote the sharing of knowledge and practices, and assess progress towards the achievements of ESD.

The 17 Sustainable Development Goals (SDGs) of the United Nations are an expression of the global resolve to create a better world by 2030. Goal 4 has specific relevance to the education policy formulation. It is an expression of the belief that it is important to, 'Ensure inclusive and equitable quality education and promote lifelong learning opportunities for all.' The ten targets included under SDG-4 clearly reveal the pivotal role of education in inclusive growth and development. Education now has to prepare and equip people to address poverty, hunger, ill-health, environment issues, climate change, gender equality, management of water and sanitation, energy issues, and several others listed among the seventeen SDGs. It has to do this so effectively, that even after leaving school or after completing higher education, the youth remain sufficiently prepared and committed to contribute effectively towards meeting the SDGs.

Reformulate Education for Sustainable Development

The contours of the post-Covid-19 world are emerging fast, so are the new challenges in every sector of human activity and endeavour that demand a new approach and innovative solutions. Changes will continue to take place in every sector, and the importance of the SDGs will harness greater attention in every sector of activity. The 17 SDGs of the 2030 UN Agenda for Sustainable Development—adopted by world leaders in September 2015 at a historic UN Summit—officially came into force on 1 January 2016. The SDGs were conceptualised at the United Nations Conference on Sustainable Development in Rio de Janeiro in 2012. The objective was to produce a set of universal goals that meet urgent environmental, political, and economic challenges. The SDGs are the blueprint to achieve a better and more sustainable future for all. They address the global challenges that we face, including those related to poverty, inequality, climate change, environmental degradation, peace and justice.

How and why did we arrive at SDGs? These goals are among the major outcomes of the global human response to tackle issues that concern everyone. No nation can ignore the plundering of natural resources by vested interests resulting in irreversible damage that creates a dark future for generations ahead. Learning to live together in a village, region, and the globe is the only alternative. SDGs are a comprehensive global initiative that guarantees victory against all that impedes the human march towards a world full of peace, dignity, and mutually respectful harmonious living. This kind of world is possible only when poverty, hunger, ill-health, and gender discrimination are discarded and the equality of opportunity, justice, and decent working conditions in the right environment are available to all. Human beings must take cognisance of climate change and take due responsibility for protecting the environment, the flora and fauna, and sea resources. All these issues and a lot more find a place in the list of SDGs. Universal education is the prime mover in each one of the 17 goals.

Universal enrolment is necessary but equally important is participation and attainment, to effectively achieve the aims of universalising good quality education. The 17 SDGs include simultaneous action in other sectors that would make life better and worth living, including alleviation of poverty and hunger, combating climate change, removal of gender bias, provision of health care, clean water, clean power, opportunities for and promotion of sustainable economic growth, productive employment, sustainable consumption patterns and other related concerns.

The Indian systems are working on all these aspects, although the progress may warrant not only additional resources but also a change in work culture. It is the pace with which initiatives—both long-term and short-term—are launched and implemented that really counts. The climate of confidence and self-assurance that was created in 2014 needs not only to be sustained, but also inspired, motivated, and wherever necessary, re-ignited. The non-utilisation of youth power is unacceptable, and every effort has to be made to give them proper education and adequate levels of skill acquisition. Creating the ministry of skill development raised high hopes among the youth. But it is felt that its plans and programme implementation strategies require much more vigour and vitality. Similarly, colleges and universities, including technical and professional institutions must respond to and face the criticism of producing 70-80 per cent graduates found deficient in the job market! Professional and academic leadership in education must rise to the occasion, fix its targets and strategies of quality improvement, curriculum renewal, and delineate the coordination of intensive emphasis on quality improvement and personality development. To achieve the global targets of the SDG-4 nationally, India must primarily focus on its teacher-education institutions. The quality of manpower in every sector is dependent on the quality of teacher-educators and teacher-education institutions. A fresh assertion of this is necessary.

There are high expectations that by 2030, complete primary and secondary education will be available for all boys and girls. There would be equal access to 'affordable vocational training', and gender and economic family disparities shall no longer remain a hindrance in the aim of achieving universal access to quality higher education. Target 4.7 of the 2030 Agenda for Sustainable Development states its purpose thus:

> By 2030, ensure that all learners acquire the knowledge and skills needed to promote sustainable development, including among others, through education for sustainable development and sustainable lifestyles, human rights, gender equality, promotion of a culture of peace and nonviolence, global citizenship and appreciation of cultural diversity and of culture's contribution to sustainable development.

It is clearly mentioned that education will achieve its objectives and goals only when adequate numbers of qualified, competent and inspired teachers are available, so Target 4 of the 2030 Agenda for Sustainable Development envisages that by 2030, there will be a substantial increase in the supply of qualified teachers through international cooperation for teacher training in developing countries, especially in the least developed countries and in small island developing states. This is a big challenge that the new policy on education in India must seriously respond to. No education policy can afford to neglect any of these aspects.

The impetus is new and timely, but the criticality of the role of education in progress and development is certainly not a new idea. The fact remains that policy makers have not focused adequate attention on the synchronisation of the content and the process of education with the delineated goals of development. This could be a consequence of lack of vision, ignorance, or absence of necessary professional support within nations. It is now widely recognised that one of the toughest crises before the newly independent nations during the last half of the 20th century was to arrive at the proper delineation of the Ideology of Progress suitable to the specific needs and requirements of the particular nation. Action plans and policies from the developed nations have often done greater damage than assisting appropriately in the march on the path of progress. There has, however, been global convergence on the idea of extending education to everyone, as the critical means of inclusive growth and development.

World Conference on Education for All (WCEFA)

WCEFA was held in Jomtien in March 1990, and it was a watershed event in the universalisation of education. The stated objective to universalise education within a decade, could not be met but the purpose of expediting educational access to all was significantly achieved. The Jomtien Declaration promising to universalise elementary education by the end of the century was a great historic landmark in extending the outreach of education to the toughest groups as well. It expedited the march towards universalising elementary education. The total enrolment rate in developing countries reached 91 per cent in 2015, with the worldwide numbering of out-of-school children dropping by half.

The World Education Forum of 2000 came out with the Dakar Declaration, in which 164 countries resolved to achieve Education for All (EFA) by 2015. Indian achievements in EFA were lauded particularly because the population has more than trebled after Independence, and we are nearing our targets of access and retention. Our previous efforts and achievements, coupled with determined new initiatives, have made India fully ready to achieve the SDGs by 2030. Our focus must be on quality, gender equality, skill acquisition, and above all, on Learning to Learn. If we have to observe a paradigm shift in one particular sector, it has to be in education, worldwide. India's new education policy can help expedite the march towards sustainable development and self-sufficiency.

Delors Commission Report of 1996

Mahatma Gandhi's seven sins find an echo in the seven tensions identified in the report to UNESCO of the International Commission on Education for the Twenty-first Century, released at the Session of the International Bureau of Education, IBE, in Geneva, on October 2, 1996, also known as the Delors Commission Report. These following seven tensions were outlined:
- global and local
- universal and individual
- traditional and modern
- long-term and short-term considerations
- need for competition and concern for opportunity
- extraordinary expansion of knowledge and the human being's capacity to assimilate
- spiritual and material

The chairperson of the Commission, Jacques Delors, clearly summarised the essence of global consultations and the future vision of global education in the twenty-first century. The report has been deliberated upon for over two decades; it has received global appreciation and has impacted policies and implementation strategies internationally.

Its articulation of the four pillars of education are:

Learning to Know: One must be familiar with the instruments of learning, which themselves may be undergoing changes and transformation. It has to be lifelong learning, and, therefore ESD includes learning to learn.

Learning to Do: Encourages skilfully accepting and performing one's own obligations—to save, nurture, and nourish the environment. Young persons need to gain formal and informal experiences, alternating with study and work.

Learning to Live Together: This was never as significant and critical as it is today, in the times of ever-growing mobility of human beings and inter-mingling of people of diverse ethnic, linguistic, religious, and cultural backgrounds. The ESD must provide opportunities to understand other people, besides equipping them with the skills of managing conflicts, and introducing concepts such as respect for pluralism, mutual respect, and peace.

Learning to Be: This is essential for personality development, the ability to act with greater autonomy, discretion, and personal responsibility. Here again, these four pillars provide the base for ESD.

Simultaneously, ESD could do much more by achieving a fifth pillar of education:

Learning to transform oneself and society, to empower people with the values and abilities to assume responsibility for creating and enjoying a sustainable future.

For the last two decades, discussions have centred on the four pillars, but the fifth one probably makes it far more comprehensive. The first UN Conference on Human Environment (UNCHE) that focussed on international environmental issues was held in Stockholm, Sweden, from January 5 to 16, 1972. In the background was a proposal made by Sweden in 1968 that the UN organise an international conference to study environmental issues, and prioritise the consensus that requires international action and cooperation. Its final declaration indicates a growing interest or concern on the finite nature of the Earth's resources, and the need for global cooperation to safeguard these, as it was the responsibility of human beings to sustain the sensitive bond between man and nature. This conference led to the creation of the United Nations Environment Programme (UNEP) in December 1972. The task assigned was to promote sustainability, and safeguard our natural habitat. The final declaration includes the importance of environmental education. The declaration had a great global impact. People began to realise and experience how rivers were getting polluted, deforestation was creating serious concerns, wildlife species were rapidly getting endangered and heading towards extinction, air pollution was getting uncontrollable, among many other related issues. Several national and global initiatives followed the Stockholm Conference. The second global environmental conference, the UN Conference on Environment and Development (UNCED) was held in Rio de Janeiro, during 3-14 June 1992.

The Brundtland Commission Report of 1987—Our Common Future—is normally considered the reference point in most of the initial deliberations on matters related to sustainable development. According to Gro Harlem

Brundtland, the former Prime Minister of Norway, 'Sustainable Development is development that meets the needs of the present without compromising the ability of future generations to meet their own needs.' This seems so very simple, as it ought to emerge from traditional wisdom. There are four dimensions of sustainable development, which can be easily comprehended: societal, environmental, cultural, and economic. These are intensely interdependent. It is also now well accepted that, 'Many crises facing the planet are interlocking crises that are elements of a single crisis of the whole.' Active human participation and endeavour are needed and all of them link seamlessly to the seventeen SDGs. The challenges of poverty, hunger, and health deserve obvious priority in global efforts. Initiatives in these three sectors require a concrete base of elementary education that was realised and resolved in March 1990 in Jomtien. The first four SDGs say it all.

ESD now needs a new generation of curricular models, textbooks, other textual materials, pedagogical initiatives, and practices. It requires both an attitudinal transformation and a pragmatic value system that appeals to the young and old alike and infuses in them, competence and a sense of commitment to contribute to the cause of sustainability. Globally, numerous initiatives are in progress, often encouraged by UN agencies, including UNESCO. The Mahatma Gandhi Institute of Education for Peace and Sustainable Development (MGIEP) established in 2012 in New Delhi as a UNESCO Grade–1 Institute is conducting several studies and initiatives on embedding ESD in textbooks. Peace and global citizenship are also included. The institute has brought together a global community of authors and practitioners, who focus on value-based and purpose-driven education. Along with eminent curriculum development experts, it prepares a curricular framework that looks at sustainable development as integral to all subjects. The outcome: *Textbooks for Sustainable Development: A Guide to Embedding* came out in 2017. It states, 'This publication is designed as a guide for stakeholders in textbook development—education ministers, national curriculum authorities, textbook writers and publishers—to help them produce a new generation of textbooks. In ESD, mere acquaintance with the problem is not sufficient, let the students and student-teachers find solutions, locate solutions, and 'live' solutions. The challenge before the teacher or teacher-educator is to engage students intellectually and emotionally in sustainable development, let them realise that the issue under consideration really matters to them. Mere intellectual awareness, and that too for just passing an examination can no more be the objective of education, and certainly not of the ESD. To achieve an attitudinal transformation is a tough task in every instance, and it applies to ESD as well.

The UNESCO-MGIEP is working on two hypotheses:
1. A whole-brain approach is necessary to produce an emotionally and intellectually resilient intellect, and
2. The education system needs to adopt the whole-brain approach.

Early findings indicate that schools adopting the whole-brain approach show promising results in producing emotionally resilient students. With the right and appropriate use of the internet, better avenues to communicate with friends, greater opportunities to co-create curriculum with the teacher could relate learning to life and more importantly, make it interesting, likeable and useful. A new climate of collaborating, and not competing could indeed lead to a peaceful and harmonious world.

Finally, we may ask: Are our educated young persons who enter various sectors fully equipped with the nuances of the national agenda of inclusive growth and development? Do we prepare them to comprehend the international scenario in their sector of activity and initiatives, and is what they study, relevant to the Indian situation? One often finds that not many teachers are really familiar even with the seventeen 'Sustainable Development Goals' identified by the UN General assembly in 2017 that are to be achieved by 2030.

Education for a Sustainable World

Envisioning the ideology of development that leads to the comprehensive progress of a nation is not an easy task. When newly independent nations went ahead with borrowed plans and programmes of development, not all of them achieved real development. Developmental strategies were invariably launched with high expectations, with the hope that these would prepare the ground for the weak, deprived, and ignored and help them lead dignified human lives, free from poverty, hunger, and ill-health. The scientific and technological advances of the twentieth century did pave the way for such a transformation. Human beings acquired knowledge, skills, and technical knowhow sufficient enough to let every human being lead a 'humane' life. Unfortunately, greed, the tendencies to accumulate and exploit natural resources, and the inadequacies inherent in plans and programmes, have by now, led to a situation in which the very existence of mankind is under threat. Thankfully, the global community is aware of the concerns and has taken several initiatives to retrieve the situation.

The UNESCO publication of 2018, *Issues and Trends in Education for Sustainable Development (ESD)*, summarises it comprehensively: 'In short, sustainable development must be integrated into education and education must be integrated into sustainable development. ESD is the holistic and transformational education and concerns learning content and outcomes, pedagogy, and the learning environment.' In essence, ESD is wholesome education that empowers and equips the learner to comprehend and put to practice, 'a balanced and integrated approach to economic, social, and environmental dimensions of sustainable development.' It is implicit that education policies and systems must transform themselves to ensure adequacy in offering knowledge, skills, values, and attitudes. These efforts need to 'Ensure inclusive and equitable quality education and promote lifelong learning opportunities for all.'

Human Development versus Environment

By 1950-60, experts and scientists began issuing a warning that developmental activity, bereft of ethical, moral, and social considerations, and oblivious of the damage it was inflicting on air, water, flora, and fauna and our total natural environment could lead to irreparable damage to the very existence of human beings. The sensitive link between man and nature was already being crushed under ever-increasing human greed, emerging out of materialistic acquisitions at the cost of spiritual pursuits. Gradually, the glitz and glare of globalisation blinded human beings to the extent that the very existence of Planet Earth is now at stake! How long can Planet Earth survive? It has been clear for a long time now that the only way to avert the assured devastation and destruction is to create global awareness; let people understand that their future is being compromised; and that the devastation can only be prevented through an attitudinal transformation! The most crucial and urgent step is to universalise elementary education. It just cannot be routine education, the rote learning of the three R's! It has to be much more than that. It has to be comprehensive education—that achieves attitudinal transformation, offers right skills and knowledge, and ensures internalisation of human values that include man's responsibility to restore and sustain man-nature mutuality.

For the first time, it was globally acknowledged that the wanton depletion of natural resources without replenishment, as was already evident globally in environmental pollution, deforestation, climate change, depletion of the Ozone layer, desertification, and so many other visible signs must be checked, and the damage repaired. Development is essential, but survival of the planet deserves primacy. Hence development has to be 'sustainable'. Its basis is indigenous knowledge, cultural comprehension, and the skills to utilise new knowledge from every source in the changing context. It has to be rooted to culture and committed to progress!

Human beings never had problems with nature as long as they respected the 'give and take' relationship between man and nature. The ancient Indian scriptures focused on this aspect in great detail, and thus all elements of nature were equated with gods! The correlation had a scientific basis, and was articulated and expressed in a manner that was easily comprehended by people at every stage. Unfortunately, over time, various aberrations and disturbances resulted in snapping of ties between people and their cultural heritage.

Invading rulers, further, left no stone unturned to destroy the natural resources of their 'colonies' to augment their own coffers. Global poverty is a creation of the materialistic pursuits and exploitative tendencies bereft of human values, compassion, fellow-feeling, and lack of respect for nature. As the disastrous consequences became more and more evident, concerns grew and serious international deliberations followed, such as the Stockholm Conference on Environment 1972, UN Conferences on Water and Desertification in 1977, the Rio Conference of 2012, the Climate Change Conference of 2015, and many more. Expediting universal education emerged very prominently every time.

Chapter 3

Transforming Higher Education: Directions and Possibilities

The educational structure that we inherited, which had been planted by foreign rulers, clearly had two strategically devastating objectives:
1. Destroy India's indigenous education system
2. Delink Indians from India

Perhaps the invaders thought, that this was the most potent strategy to subjugate India. There were clear-cut evangelical objectives as well. It was also implicit that the, 'Souls of the Savages' would be redeemed, and there would be no idol worshippers left in India once the new education system took root. One could not ignore the wicked stratagem and its destructive outcome, in which the British succeeded, probably even beyond their expectations. The biggest problem was when initially, India decided to continue with the inherited system, and did not have the courage to replace it with an indigenous system. The country's education policy continued with the Commonwealth link, overlooking to a great extent, the great tradition of our knowledge quest, the insight in spirituality and astrophysics, philosophy, the sciences, and so many other areas of knowledge. India stretched the education system that was strategically designed, to educate just a few for specific tasks, to universalise education. The entire system was shattered, credibility lost, and quality severely diluted.

In a democratic set-up, with all of its contextual diversities, once a new policy is announced, debate is inevitable. Furthermore, criticism is not necessarily professional and objective; the presence of ideological considerations and political inclinations is noticeable. I have observed this phenomenon for over fifty years, and found it highly educative. As one of the persons responsible for preparing the new Curriculum Framework for School Education (NCFSE), that was released on 14 November 2000, I faced its full fury. The NCFSE was not a comprehensive education policy document, but had the potential to bring about tangible and significant changes in school education, and that, by implication and extension, meant transformation in the entire education scenario in India. The Framework was prepared after a nation-wide process of consultation in which every sector was invited to participate. It was strongly voiced that India needed a curriculum that was rooted to the Indian soil, its history, heritage, and culture, and was strongly committed to receive and generate new knowledge.

Things have changed in the modern world and India and Indians are merged into this modernisation. The knowledge quest is now often pursued with the sole and primary commercial considerations, whether it is getting a patent first or taking over the market! Historical interventions impeded Indian knowledge traditions, and today, we are just copying the trends of much-glamourised globalisation. We appear to be passing through an era of selfish weakness instead of sincere, committed and selfless pursuits of new knowledge. A course correction is urgently required. Essentially, it amounts to broadening the vision of the knowledge quest that India must articulate in the current-day idiom, accept and implement.

Education for Learning to Live Together

One of the pillars of education as stated in the Delors Commission Report was that education in the twenty-first century would be about 'Learning to Live Together'. This is now the critical component of education and learning globally as people are moving to alien locations and are destined to live together with people who may be vastly different in their social, economic, cultural and religious backgrounds.

The freedom of expression constitutes the backbone of people's faith in a democratic process. This also permits organised protests on issues that indicate differences between governments and certain sections of the people. Anti-social groups and individuals with vested interests invariably infiltrate such organised protests, and often succeed in misleading sensitive and young persons in colleges and universities. Small-time politicians never miss such opportunities of adding fuel to the fire. Educated young people taking recourse to organised violence and destroying public property is totally unacceptable in functional democracies. This then plays on the behaviour and psyche of young minds. Students get influenced and adversely affected. In the final analysis, education takes a back seat. The youth of today have to learn to live together with diversities in most countries and India is no exception. In fact, many European nations look towards India to learn how it has functioned so effectively for thousands of years with adherents of different faiths and religions. Our young people must learn to celebrate diversity. They must also realise how deeply endowed the culture of ancient India was that it recognised the essential unity of all human beings, and propagated that every religion must get equal respect from the followers of other religions, as there can be different and divergent paths to reach the same Ultimate Truth. There is no other way than the culture of the acceptance of diversity.

In India, education is subsidised by the taxpayer, as almost 80 per cent of the Indian population continues to live below the poverty line. It is unimaginable and unacceptable that public property be vandalised by people who love India and Indians. This thought process has to be revived in the minds of students. Our education system has to take note of the bigger picture as it readies the next generation to take over the reins of the nation. Education planning must extend its canvas beyond the mere completion of courses and gauging the percentage of marks the students score in board examinations. It is a serious inadequacy of school education if dynamic teenagers who enter higher education institutes (HEIs) are bereft of social and national responsibility and easily become pawns in the hands of a few unsocial and unscrupulous elements in creating disturbances and destruction. While law-enforcing agencies need to take immediate steps to check violence and destruction, the keepers and makers of education policies must ponder over long-term strategies.

Educational Institutions Must Look Within

Central Universities and other national level institutions of higher learning and research must regularly ask: Are we equipped to take a fresh look? An institution can play a leadership role only if it collectively comprehends the dynamic nature of its mission, objectives and goals in professional terms, and consistently strives to understand the import of 'looking within'! National-level institutions must remain ever-alert on 'growing up' professionally. Reputations are made only through the persistence of single-minded commitment to the cause over a long period of time. When academics within an institution get divided on ideological constraints, there is a drastic reduction in time available for high quality, collaborative research and genuine innovations. In post-Independence India, the country witnessed the sharp decline of some of its prestigious learning centres of earlier years.

One of the most prestigious national institutions of India, Jawaharlal Nehru University (JNU) in New Delhi, has often been in a state of ferment and turbulence. For the common man, unfortunately, JNU has become known more for its protests, slogans, and agitations than for its outstanding professional and academic contribution or its impact on major policy formulations. The problem in JNU culture, apparently is the limited or no scope for healthy dialogue or debate. If it were so, JNU could have become a place of pilgrimage for genuine scholars from India and abroad. In fact, the level of investment that the nation has made in this one university, makes it obligatory on the part of the university to prove worthy of the confidence imposed in it. It is in the fitness of things if JNU and other dynamic Institutes for Higher Learning come forward with a model for re-engineering quality enhancement strategies.

The growth of an unbiased and pure professional tradition of the knowledge quest suffers in the face of severe apathy towards indigenous traditions of knowledge creation and dissemination, the essence of which may still be relevant. It is globally acknowledged that education in every country must be rooted in culture and committed to progress. Education has suffered because of the lack of courage to link it to the national tradition of growth, knowledge, and scholarship instead of an overdependence on our inherited legacy. It should never be difficult for a professional and unbiased educationist to conclude that education in every country must be a product of an indigenous thought process and appropriate new scientific knowledge. Consequently, the first requirement at the policy planning level is absolute familiarity with the indigenous traditions of the knowledge quest, its creation, generation, transfer, and utilisation. This is a necessary but not a closed exercise. It is equally necessary to acquire deep comprehension of new knowledge that could be available from all possible sources and places.

Social cohesion and religious amity has to be cemented in India; it is a core element of economic growth, progress, and development. The tradition of dialogue and communication has always been the hallmark of knowledge growth and it is ever more relevant and necessary in present times. Our institutes of learning, schools and universities must focus purely on the quest of knowledge for fulfilling the aspirations of the youth and the nation.

The Ethos of Quality Erosion in Education

It is a common lament that Indian universities do not figure prominently in global institutional rankings. Serious concerns are often expressed on the decline in quality education across the board. The apparent dismal performance of learner achievements in government schools is regularly highlighted by several surveys that have acquired credibility over the years, and this includes Pratham's Annual Status of Education Report (ASER). Some pertinent questions are:

1. How can the education system be reformed so as to address increasing unemployment among educated young people?
2. To what extent will steps like the creation of the Ministry of Skill Development and Entrepreneurship help?
3. What needs to be done to restore the credibility and public acceptance of the current education system?

India has reached a stage when parents want to educate their children—both boys and girls, in good schools, which in the current context denotes a private school. If around 60 per cent students are still in government schools, it is only because the parents are either unable to afford the 'luxury' of a private school; or location-wise there is none available; or the parent is in a rapidly transferable job and shifting from one private school to another is not viable. In higher education, the competition is too tough to get admission into reputed public-funded professional institutions. Private institutions are expensive. Therefore, those who can afford it, look for good quality education overseas. As the demands have increased, several States have quietly withdrawn, paving the way for the private entrepreneur both in school education and in the higher education sector (HES).

India began with around fifty universities in 1950. In 2020, there were over a thousand universities, which included state and central universities, deemed universities, private universities and institutes of national importance which include the IIMs and IITs, among others. There are around forty-five thousand colleges. This growth is undoubtedly a great achievement. However, besides the dilution in the quality of education, the value system in educational institutions is also apparently compromised. To recall a somewhat similar situation and its analysis, one could refer to John W. Gardner's book, *Excellence: Can we be equal and excellent too*? Referring to overemphasis on attending colleges and universities, Gardner summarises in his essay,

> The crowding in our colleges is less regrettable than the confusion in our values. Human dignity and worth should be assessed only in terms of those qualities of mind and spirit that are within the reach of every human being. If we assume that college is the sole cradle of human dignity, need we be surprised that everyone wants to be rocked in that cradle?

He elaborates that the intention is not to undervalue the achievements and importance of higher education but to remember that it alone need not become the sole criterion of assessing human worth. We get a much better comprehension of missing elements in Indian education if we reflect on how gradual decline or change altered the emphasis on the total worth of the individual. There are occasions when personal experiences reflect the prevalent institutional ethos, and that could lead to tangible reforms without the need for illusive fiscal inputs.

A Case Study

In 1962, obtaining an M Sc degree in Physics with electronics as a special paper was one of the most sought after courses offered by the University of Allahabad. Just before the start of preparation leave for the final examination, Professor Krishna took stock of how much of the course had been covered. He was a highly respected academic, known internationally for having established the microwave laboratory, which at that stage was a pioneering effort. One of the chapters on 'Detectors' had not been covered in the regular class teaching, and therefore, students were sure it would not feature in the examination paper. When the Professor realised this, he asked the group to assemble the following day. 'Detectors' were taught for four hours that day, followed by another three hours the next day. All the students were now convinced that at least one question on 'Detectors' would certainly appear in the examination paper. But that was not the case; there was no question on 'Detectors'.

After about three years, at a tea gathering, someone, hesitatingly recalled how 'Detectors' had not been detected in that particular examination! Five of that original group of fifteen students were now research scholars, and they like the others, eagerly waited for Professor Krishna's response. He revealed: 'I was the paper setter that year. I knew there were no questions on 'Detectors'. But, how could anyone get a degree of M Sc Physics, with specialisation in Electronics, from the University of Allahabad, and not have learnt enough about 'Detectors'?'

He reiterated how the University had gained its reputation and credibility and how the Department of Physics had to maintain its standards. He mentioned how the professors of the Department had professional, moral, and ethical obligations. He also recalled how he had been advised in his early learning years by his favourite teacher, never to enter a classroom if not dutifully prepared.

He shared an invaluable lesson with his students–never use old notes and prepare afresh each time, even if one was teaching the same topic in two different sections! Then he gently pulled out two sheets of paper from his pocket: his notes for the first-year undergraduate class that he had taken that morning. He had been teaching for about thirty years and could easily teach even postgraduate students continuously for three to four hours without any notes or books; yet he was following the advice of his teacher so sincerely, even at that stage! He was an exemplar of teacher education for prospective teachers; this was value education, and a measure of quality university teaching in higher education.

The Department of Physics of the University of Allahabad was reputed to work 24X7. At any time in the night, a couple of youngsters would be always working in the laboratory. There was no mandate to do so, and no recording of attendance. Values were learnt because these were practiced in the department by all the seniors. The quality of education can only improve when the situation is analysed and inferences drawn, regardless of ideological constraints. An important factor was that the university system did not face the challenge of vacant academic posts in universities in that era. Whenever there was a vacancy, heads of departments were authorised to make ad hoc arrangements. In due course, the new faculty member got the appointment letter from the Registrar's office, with all the pay and allowances according to norms. There was no system of guest lecturers, or lecture-wise payment system. Every senior academic was available to provide the necessary inspiration, motivation, and guidance to a new entrant.

However, things are very different in present times and several departments may not even have one-third of the teachers, as per the sanctioned posts. It is common knowledge that in most State universities, Vice-Chancellors have to seek permission of the government to appoint teachers, even for sanctioned academic posts.

This has negatively impacted institutions in more than one way and highlighted that the role of academic leadership just cannot be ignored.

Equality of Opportunity and Talent Nurturance

Democratic education systems talk of the equality of opportunity and of access and success to every child. This generates high hopes and kindles aspirations, particularly amongst the weaker sections of society that have waited for generations for a better and dignified quality of life. The first requirement has been a Common School System (CSS), which ensures that:

1. No child is denied admission in any school in the vicinity of his or her home, irrespective of social or economic background.
2. Individual attention is given to each child. The child's interests must be kept in mind; creativity and curiosity should not be hampered.
3. An inviting learning environment is created by competent and committed teachers.
4. A balanced teacher-student ratio is maintained.

The education system could not prevent the decline of credibility and acceptability of government schools, as the essential spirit of CSS was ignored. While it was prominently included in the National Policy on Education 1968, and CSS did find a place in subsequent policies of 1986 and 1992 as well, the system was not effectively implemented. Government schools are now patronised only by those who have no other alternative, either because of their meagre economic resources, or non-availability of a private school nearby. Often, working people with transferable jobs are forced to patronise government schools. A feeble attempt was made in the Right to Education Act of 2009 to reserve 25 per cent seats in the lower classes for children of weaker sections. However, a majority of the schools managed to find their ways out of this commitment.

When the first batch of children admitted under this category, in 2010 completed Class 8, the schools insisted that they pay the regular school fee. This was quite devastating both psychologically and emotionally for the students and their families. Around 60 to 65 per cent of school children still study in government schools, which are invariably deficient in infrastructure, teachers, learning materials, and are lacking in other basic professional requirements. Therefore, most surveys and studies on the outcomes indicate low learner achievements, and a consistent and steady annual decline. The silver lining is that despite such a high percentage of children completing their schooling under limited conditions with severe impediments, and only a small number getting into higher education institutions (HEIs), our educated young students are highly sought after in other countries and are offered really challenging assignments that they invariably complete superbly, bringing prestige and praise to India. However, there is a dimmer picture within the country. Graduates from coveted HEIs, specialising in technical and management education, are often found lacking in their readiness to accept responsibility in the job market. This happens because the foundation of their early years is weak. The basic responsibility is to ensure good quality school education which is favourably comparable in higher education. Once access and participation in education is ensured with adequate professional and infrastructural inputs, the issue of nurturing individual talent deserves attention. It is accepted or believed that the marks obtained in the board examination do not guarantee total personality development and specialised talent. Teachers can be entrusted to ascertain the appropriate path of passage to excellence in students. Identifying aptitude and talent, and developing meaningful personality traits has to be a continuous process that must begin very early. The foremost national priority for the investment of public funds must be teacher-education and school education. This would ensure the highest level of returns.

Simultaneously, talent must be located and nurtured. In the Indian psyche, the commercialisation of education is unacceptable, and must be strongly discouraged. Education is still the only ray of hope for the weaker sections. We must now accept that knowledge, both secular and temporal, has been created and discovered in all parts of the Globe, although times, measures, and magnitudes could differ. Ancient Indians had really toiled hard on the terrain of the knowledge quest, and had earned respect from all over. Are we doing so now? This aspect should be paramount in present-day considerations. The strife-torn world of today should be looking towards India, conscious of its unique historical standing as a nation that has held together over centuries with every conceivable diversity, like that of ethnicity, language, religion, and culture. The West is now facing the problems arising out of the necessity to learn to live together with such diversities.

Education for Civil Behaviour

The churning in the changing socio-economic and cultural aspects of human life is part of human civilisation. The pace of change in almost every aspect of human life being experienced at present, has no parallel in human history. In fact, the twentieth century is known as the century of change, particularly in view of the advances in science and of human understanding of the forces of nature. It was the one common factor in every narration to refer to the impact of science, technology, and industry on society, family, and individual human beings. The twentieth century also witnessed the elimination of colonialism and imperialism and this led to the universal acceptance of the people's democratic movement. Power shifted from hierarchical transition and ascendance to elected representatives of the people. The strength of the Indian democracy was universally acknowledged as it has consistently ensured the smooth transition of power to the elected representative without any third-party intervention.

One can always approach knowledgeable persons who have witnessed every general election held in India over the past 75 years; and who have keenly observed the change that has taken place in the very concept of an elected representative of the people. They are best suited to articulate how over decades, a paradigm shift has taken place in how people measure these *netas* (political leaders), and how these *netas* relate to their electors! Exceptions apart, electors have now even been voting for known criminals and for those who have amassed wealth shamelessly; and even those known not to care for the very people who elect them as legislators.

The ways that the legislators and the Parliament function have also undergone a complex transition and a huge behavioural transformation. I wonder whether anyone can say that he or she is proud of it? I recall how my young friends and I, in the University of Allahabad in the 1950s and 1960s bristled at the comments that Winston Churchill had made about Indians before Independence. We had at that time great enlightened leadership, devoted to the national cause, men and women who had sacrificed everything during the freedom struggle. But Churchill's reported comments were:

> Power will go into the hands of rascals, rogues, freebooters, all Indian leaders will be of low calibre and men of straw. They will have sweet tongues and silly hearts. They will fight amongst themselves for power and India will be lost in political squabbles. A day would come when even air and water would be taxed in India.

The Preamble to the Constitution of UNESCO declares, 'Since wars begin in the minds of men, it is in the minds of men that the defences of peace must be constructed.' Further, 'UNESCO works to create the conditions for dialogue among civilizations, cultures and people, based upon respect for commonly shared values.' UNESCO identifies itself with the people throughout the globe, and assists interaction, cooperation and collaboration to formulate and implement plans and programmes that will help achieve sustainable development, goals that would include observance of human rights, alleviation of poverty, hunger and ill-health. It works through interactions, studies, and through its

works in education, sciences, culture, communication, and information. Its overall objectives include:
1. Attaining quality education for all and lifelong learning.
2. Mobilising science, knowledge and policy for sustainable development.
3. Addressing emerging social and ethical challenges.
4. Fostering cultural diversity, intercultural dialogue and a culture of peace.
5. Building inclusive knowledge societies through information and communication.

Clearly, all five of these objectives are interlinked and also interdependent. Attaining these objectives depends on the readiness of 'man' to play his part in creating a world of peace, tranquillity, dignity, and acceptance of diversity. In Indian culture, it could be the acceptance of the presence of divinity in everyone.

The 'Me Too' protests that emerged strongly in 2020-2021, in India were an eyeopener. It was an issue that drew the attention of every one, every woman, and every man who respects women. The categoric statements made by working women against well-known individuals and the responses they generated opened a Pandora's box, especially for the parents of young women, who are particularly worried about their school-and college-going daughters, working spouses, and all the female members of the family who now move out and interact with people in various places. While the spotlight fell more on a very specific sector, the media and film industry, it was well-accepted that the problem was more universal in nature. While it was also accepted that there are always two sides to every coin, but the hue and cry on this very real problem was unprecedented.

Education Must Acculturate

Practically every day we see reports on sexual harassment, suicides, acid attacks, and read about rape and murders. The shocking aspect is that cases of sexual harassment even in so-called prestigious schools, institutions, and universities have been on the rise, but these are invariably treated in a 'routine' manner. Young people suffer on grounds other than gender discrimination as well. In institutes of higher education, cases of sexual harassment are not uncommon. In addition, there is rampant political exploitation of the youth. Every positive step and innovation introduced to curb the menace of gender discrimination, more often than not, falls victim to ideological moorings and other disruptive and destructive elements. The relatively recent illustrative example takes us back to the most liberally invested university, JNU, as described earlier. It has apparently and rather consistently, been high-jacked by a group of ideologically constrained individuals who have gone out of their way to make it a hub of political activism. In the name of free-play of ideas, they ensured that only like-minded individuals could enter their inner circle. Now that some cracks are appearing in their well-protected citadel of power and authority, these elements are obviously, deeply upset.

This is a rare university in many ways. One could remain a research scholar there for umpteen years, pursuing a PhD for ages, enjoying the facilities and fellowship at the expense of the tax-payer. And, believe me, they do all this to better the lot of the 'last man in the line'! No regulations as applicable to other universities are acceptable. If they wish to go on an election campaign for three or four months, no questions could be asked; they would make it seem as if their perks and fellowship amount was untouchable. Their reasoning was that we are JNU, we are distinct, different, and distinguished! Their ideology was that our goal in the name of the welfare of the proletariat, is the destruction of the existing system of governance, culture, and social mores. These no-attendance-no-regulation seekers are probably not aware that institutions cannot survive on past reputation alone, and that they have to consistently project dynamism to keep pace with changes, as well as have the ability to analyse these changes and envision their future implications. The requirement is to come out with a well-studied response for the benefit of the people and the nation.

Reference is often made to the landmark judgment of the SCI delivered in 1997 in the Vishaka case. It laid down guidelines to be followed by every establishment in a sexual harassment complaint at the workplace. The Sexual Harassment Act of 2013 casts several obligations on the employer, the most important being to provide a safe working environment. Essentially, the Act and the earlier guidelines were attempts to, 'Provide for the effective enforcement of the basic human right of gender equality and guarantee against sexual harassment and abuse, more particularly against sexual harassment at the workplace.'

The UGC-issued guidelines to universities and other institutions were meant to create a permanent mechanism to ensure that the SCI guidelines are effectively implemented. Every institution is obliged to constitute a committee as per the guidelines and notify it to all concerned. While the mechanism exists, its efficacy needs thorough scrutiny. For years together, such cases remained under or uninvestigated, causing tremendous mental trauma to the victims. Punishment, if at all awarded, is rarely commensurate with the magnitude of the crime or offence. The fact remains that most of the institutions have not implemented the provisions and have not acted in accordance with the true spirit of ensuring an environment free from even the apprehension of sexual harassment. Probably, some more steps are required to ensure that every educational institution pays greater attention to the concerns of gender equality and to the elimination of practices that hurt beyond acceptance in an acculturated society, and inflict irreparable damage on the psyche and personality of the victim. Universities like JNU, BHU, and IGNOU must become the torch-bearers in eliminating sexual harassment from their campus.

The gradual erosion of an empathetic traditional teacher-taught relationship of mutual affection and the highest level of consideration, care, and respect between the two stands visibly weakened. It is often manifesting in several tragic events that are reported rather regularly from different places and stages in education. The sublime components of the hallowed teacher-taught relationship are withering away under the glare and glamour of globalisation, liberalisation, and commercialisation. While talking to a group of teachers and reminding them that they should consider themselves blessed for the opportunity of creating the future of India by getting the chance to reshape the lives of thousands of young persons, they just look at each other nonchalantly and get ready to opt out of the gathering. Some of them appear to be in a hurry to cater to their additional income by taking up additional tuition or duties in a coaching institution! They are simply not interested in any motivational, or even in an 'impractical philosophical discourse'! In the 1950s-1960s, it was almost unthinkable for a university or college teacher conducting tuition classes or extending his or her services to a commercial coaching institution. Today, it has become acceptable!

This is the current trend and to change this system or to bring about a reversal, ground realities must first be acknowledged. A rise in the credibility of prestigious institutions delivers exponential developmental outcomes. Presently, in the first quarter of the twenty-first century, it is also the pace of science that attracts attention in every discourse. References to ICT and Nano technology overwhelm every policy, plan, and programme that aims at progress and development.

Elements of Educational Change

The foundation for a new education system must rest on several factors that deeply influence learning—good teachers, dynamic curriculum, and an emotional bond between the teachers, the learners, and the educational institutes. Education systems are stressed, even in educationally developed societies as education is a dynamic process, and must keep pace both with the changing expectations of society and emerging aspirations of the young.

In India, as in most nations that were caught in a foreign yoke for centuries, education received new impetus in the last five decades. This was more so after the World Conference on Education, held in Jomtien, Thailand, in March 1990, that resolved to universalise elementary education in the next 10 years with extensive global collaboration. India can justifiably boast of its achievement in widening access to education to the remotest hill and tribal area. It required extensive efforts, plans, and programmes to reach an estimated enrolment of over 96 per cent, despite a population increase of more than three times. India now has around 1.5 million schools and over 230 million children enrolled in them. This is not a mean achievement for a country that began its educational reformation after Independence in extremely difficult conditions, with a literacy rate of less than 20 per cent, and huge paucity of resources, both in qualified people and teaching material.

While the expansion of access meant opening more schools, at a pretty fast pace, there was a serious dearth of trained teachers and of the capacity of the states to provide optimum infrastructural support. Things, however, did move. One of the biggest and most tangible achievements was attitudinal transformation. Every community, social and cultural group, realises only now, the importance and value of quality education for their children, including for both boys and girls. The Gen Next of today may find it strange to comprehend that to prepare people to send their daughters to school was a daunting task during the first four decades after Independence. Even today, in several remote areas and with certain sections of people, the slogan, *Beti bachao, beti padhao* (save the daughter, educate the daughter) is broadcast.

Before the National Policy on Education, 1968, it was accepted that girls were not fit to study science and mathematics and were generally encouraged to take up vocations like spinning and weaving, or subjects like home science, or social sciences only. Because of visionary educationists, under the leadership of Prof. D. S. Kothari, the National Commission on Education (1964-66), recommended compulsory teaching of science and mathematics to both boys and girls till they completed 10 years of schooling. This is certainly one of the historic examples of dynamism needed in education, its policies and implementation.

The infrastructure of schools, the inclusion of extensive

laboratories and the intent and process of education and teaching have undergone significant changes. From the *Tat-Patti* (narrow jute floor mats or covering) stage, India has rapidly transitioned to smart classrooms. The contrast however, remains, between the metropolitan urban and very remote rural scenarios. Dynamic systems cannot afford lethargy or systemic slumber to relax and gloat over achievements. Every issue resolved and every problem tackled generates new challenges.

The Indian education system is no exception, and we can list a plethora of issues and concerns that demand urgent remediation. It is because of such imperatives in educational advancement that the educational curriculum requires consistent review and revision. It requires regular surveys, studies, and research to point out what needs to be changed, discarded or deleted, and added or augmented.

Normally, at the very least, a five-year cycle is considered necessary to incorporate curricular reforms in school education. Textbooks are revised after renewing the curriculum and re-formulating the syllabi. Certain alert systems do realise that the pace of change is so fast that a five-year cycle may be too slow in comparison and, therefore, frontline curricula are provided for, and incorporated with broader guidelines and made available to schools and teachers. This interim corrective system takes care of urgent requirements and students are not deprived of new developments, changes or innovations.

In India, over 50 school boards are authorised to prepare their own curricula, syllabi, and generate appropriate textbooks and all boards must prepare students for national-level competitions. This means that students from different boards must come with an equally similar educational background. As already stated, NCERT, is mandated to prepare school curricula and related textbooks in consultation with State agencies, and it is up to State governments to either adopt them as they are or prepare their own textbooks incorporating local elements wherever necessary. However, they are mandated to retain information, which is of national and global relevance.

NCERT books should normally be accepted as the only exclusive textbooks for every subject. Take the example of environmental education. Content for different geographical locations must necessarily be different, for example in Tripura and Thiruvananthapuram, but the NCERT textbook will offer guidance in maintaining the level and standard, apart from providing essential general information. At this stage, even curriculum developers and textbook writers require regular in-service orientation on how things are being analysed and included in an era characterised by information and communication technology (ICT).

Teacher-student equation: A textbook is no longer the only source of information available to a student. Nevertheless, it is universally acknowledged that despite all that is now available to the learner, courtesy ICT, Internet and ever-improving gadgets, a personalised teacher-learner relationship is always necessary to ensure valuable human interaction in the overall growth of the learner. Every teacher has to remain aware and realise that life-long learning is vital to remain relevant in the profession. Only such teachers who practice what they preach can impress upon their students the real significance of 'life-long learning'.

Only with such a vision, can an alert teacher be in a position to nurture the inbuilt creativity and curiosity in every child. It is no longer essential to impart everything within the classroom. Teachers now support and encourage students to search other sources of information, learn how to sift that information and absorb what is relevant to increase knowledge and develop skills. In the process, a teacher educates the student in learning to learn a skill that must necessarily be acquired during schooling.

As the learners move upwards on the learning curve, they need a much more flexible and personalised curriculum, because this is critical for self-learning, self-actualisation, and optimising their potential. The motivation and inspiration comes from committed and performing teachers who can assist learners in developing comprehensive abilities to enable them to creatively contribute to the socio-economic, cultural, political, and technological sectors. This is possible only when the teacher-training institutions also realise and accept their transformed role now known as 'multiple intelligence'.

Teachers are no longer mere transactors of textual material within classrooms. They are appreciators, guides, counsellors, moulders, instructors, and much more. They are the first icons and exemplars after the child's parents. Only such teachers can succeed in the future who realise the criticality of their persona in the lives of their young learners.

Easy access to schooling: What is more critical to a community than the availability of a functional school nearby? This situation has deteriorated gradually and has reached rather disturbing proportions. Textbooks, teachers, the Internet and other aspects come later, and a physical educational institute, a school, is the most essential. Several State governments are now 'merging' thousands of schools, especially those located in far-flung, rural, tribal, and hilly areas with nearby schools to make them viable. When a school has an enrolment of less than 10 or 20 students, its continuation may not be considered viable in routine economic planning, consideration, but should that be the only criterion? It has to be very demoralising and demotivating for children whose school is shifted to another place.

Traditionally, India has successfully experimented with various models of schooling during the nation's early years. Now that educated and literate persons are available in almost every habitation and village, these models other than what is demanded in the Right to Education Act (RTE Act) of 2009, could also be tried to ensure that no children drop out of school because of the merger and assimilation of 'their' school. Good education requires good teachers, a dynamic curriculum, and an emotional bond between teachers, learners and their school.

Revitalising Distraught Education Systems

The quality of education and the suitability of its products determines the efficacy and pace of progress and development in various sectors of growth and advancement. While no one doubts the sincerity of initiatives, plans and programmes launched from time to time, these are often impeded by certain practices that have gained ground over the years because of unscrupulous elements in the education sector. A couple of decades ago, realising the gravity of the damage caused by mass copying in examinations, the Uttar Pradesh government issued a *nakal-virodhi* ordinance (to prevent copying). It had its impact. However, it was repealed by their successors, a government, known to be soft towards the examinees.

The malpractice has since grown to gigantic proportions, both in UP and Bihar. Sadly enough, mass copying in examinations, making degrees available for a consideration, and 'fixing' of examination sectors, have not only ruined the future prospects of millions of young people, but have also contributed to the decline of the credibility of the certificates, diplomas and degrees awarded by some of the institutions in these states. Improving the quality of education in these two states remains a daunting task. A news item, 'UP School Board examinees dip by 9 lakhs for the 2018-19 examinations' was like a red flag. Normally, the numbers of those taking exams increase every year in proportion with the growing population.

This unexpected and significant decrease deserves serious analysis by experts as it shows the dampening aspirations of the young on the one hand, and the dream of this being the 'Age of demographic dividends for the youngest nation', on the other! During 2017-18, around 11 lakh students, although registered, dropped out of the UP Board examinations of class 10 and 12! The pass percentage was 75.16 in high school and 72.43 in intermediate. Around 27 lakh young students failed in one year in one state. On the very first day of the examinations, in 2017-18, around 1.8 lakh examinees reportedly abstained, including 1.27 lakh from class 12.

The numbers have been increasing. The new state government had put in place strict measures to confront the *nakal* (copying) *mafia*, and it made all the difference. The moot point is that the *nakal mafia* did not acquire this 'strength, power, and credibility' amongst the masses on its own. The obvious inference was its prior collusion with politicians and bureaucrats. It is encouraging that now the number of those purchasing certificates of success, are declining.

In 2015 visuals of copying in board examinations from Vaishali of Bihar were quite horrifying. Parents and students scaled walls, several fake examiners were detected, and finally some thousand students were expelled. In the case of the VYAPAM examination, admission, and recruitment scam in Madhya Pradesh in 2013, scamsters, including politicians, senior and junior officials, and businessmen were caught employing imposters to write papers, manipulate seating arrangements in examination halls and provide forged answer sheets by bribing officials. VYAPAM is the state government's self-financed and autonomous body responsible for conducting various entrance examinations. It is widely believed that scandalous practices in entry to medical colleges and in recruitment to state government jobs have continued unchecked for several years! All those who could purchase entry are said to have walked into the precincts of much-sought-after medical colleges! Generations of young students have suffered injustice at the hands of corrupt officials and politicians in positions of power.

This destruction of values and harm bestowed on the younger generations was not limited to UP and Bihar only. It extends to most parts of the country. The original *nakal mafia* nexus now extends to several other sectors dealing with young people and their future. Some coaching institutions have been caught leaking exam papers just to showcase a high success result in professional entrance tests. These groups have even created links with public-service commissions, and teacher-recruitment commissions. If social consciousness and awareness disappears entirely from the human psyche, it can cause irreparable damage, especially to the young generation. Such issues, where the interest is to make money at any cost, pose a great challenge to the education system of the country.

If the reduced number of examinees in UP is any indication, we can hardly envisage how many lakhs of our youth are regular victims of this unscrupulous exploitation. The situation is further accentuated by several other factors—ten lakh posts of school teachers in government schools lying vacant, a huge upsurge of private teacher education institutions; uncontrollably high-fee charging 'public schools' indulging in rampant commercialisation; and the loss of credibility of government schools. One can safely say, however, that there are no issues with about 30 per cent of children and young students who are fortunate to get a good level of education in prestigious and elite private and government schools.

There is another side to the same coin. Among those thirty per cent students that qualify from Indian schools, are those whose academic acumen is considered good enough for them to get admission, even scholarships into well-known HEIs overseas. Our quest is to keep them back here to study further in HEIs in India. Many students from other countries also seek admission into India's HEIs. Young Indians have excelled practically in every field of ICT, space sciences, and in every promising area that could change the world for the better. Good quality education, presently available roughly only to about one-third of India's students, needs to be extended to all, and extended fast.

Educationally alert countries are conscious of the pace of change all around, and the need to prepare their young generation for a highly competitive world. While we need to combat prevailing malpractices in India's education system, we need to also look around and observe how conditions are being improved globally. Like other educationally advanced nations, we must put into practice the adage that investment in education pays the highest returns. No nation can afford to be slow and reticent on this count. Renowned columnist Thomas Friedman in his 2016 book, *Thank You for Being Late* comprehends the pace of unprecedented changes taking place all around, calling the present times as the 'age of accelerations'! Even if India is late on certain counts of efficacy and improvement, it must continue to invigorate the system with new ideas and initiatives.

Building Educational Institutions

It is now widely recognised that India must have a presence among the international rankings of HEIs. In pursuance of its decision to move ahead in this direction, the Central government has identified six institutions that get this tag initially. It would be increased to twenty in due course. However, academics with no ideological baggage and political aspirations insist that the issue is not that of creating the twenty top institutions but of checking the downward slide practically in every professional aspect of most of the universities funded by the State and Central Governments. India certainly has more than twenty institutions/universities that are really of global standards but may not find a place in rankings that are based upon specific cultural context and scale, the origin of which could be traced to the impact of globalisation, privatisation, and commercialisation.

There is a strong school of thought that suggests that India, with its commitment to provide 'inclusive education' to everyone, including to 50 per cent of those who need reservations, would do better to concentrate on quality upgradation across the board than in joining the race for a place in the global ranking list. This must include school education as well. It is an encouraging fact that despite all the deficiencies in our education system, our young graduates have brought great recognition and reputation to themselves through their presence in NASA in the earlier years and then extended this to their tangible presence in Silicon Valley! While this is exemplary, we cannot ignore the stark reality of the reports that over 80-90 per cent of professional graduates are not found fit for the job market even in India! The reason for this needs incisive analysis. We have them all—the very good institutions, some mediocre institutions, and then, even worse institutions created through private intrusion of those for whom education is just another industry that offers assured and increasing dividends. The system just cannot be improved upon by merely concentrating on the twenty lucky institutions who will be lucky enough to be placed on a global list, while ignoring the vast numbers of others.

To understand the downward slide of the quality in Indian education, once again we need to recall the conditions that prevailed in schools, colleges, and universities just 50 to 60 years ago. Several universities like those of Calcutta, Delhi, Bombay, Madras, Patna, Allahabad, and Varanasi were known for their professional contributions and enjoyed great credibility. Government schools in every district and government colleges also enjoyed high credibility and were sought after by children from every strata of society. While there were instances of school teachers taking tuition classes, it was unthinkable that a college teacher or university professor would take tuition or associate himself or herself with a coaching institute. But the prevailing conditions were bad. Teachers were poorly paid and the fate of university teachers was not far better. Infrastructure facilities were inadequate. But none of this dampened the enthusiasm and commitment of teachers in schools and university. To cite an example, the science faculty of the University of Allahabad located at the Muir Central College, was known for its maximum contributions to the civil services and for high-class contributions in scientific research at the international level; infrastructurally however, they had only one telephone connection in the Office of the Dean of the Faculty. Any professor missing a class was unthinkable. Every faculty member considered it a moral and divine obligation to ensure that the desired extent and level of learning was indeed imparted to every learner. Academics conducted high-level research as one of their major pursuits without needing extra incentives, instigations, or compulsions.

Everyone successfully aspired to publish his or her contribution in the best and most reputed journals. There always were exceptions, of course, but that did not impact the overall work culture, professional commitment, or the quality of products and research output. Work ethics and commitment were not limited by the clock. This area of activity has apparently since shifted to coaching institutions, committee membership of regulatory bodies, foreign trips, and much more. Great institutions create a work-culture of their own. It is domain knowledge forcing academics to 'think' and that takes time. Sadly, the bureaucracy in India takes decisions based on recommendations by academics. Since domain knowledge is not of much consequence to the former, the very essence of autonomy is lost.

The Indian Institutes of Technology (IITs) and Indian Institutes of Management (IIMs) have gained stature and recognition and managed autonomy to a great extent. The government has assured that it will gradually extend the trend not only to twenty institutions of eminence but also to other universities and colleges. It is intriguing however, to learn that several colleges are not willing to accept autonomy, a fact that indicates the complexity of the Indian academic world. Autonomy obviously means greater responsibility, accountability, and greater effort to stay effective in the world of creating new knowledge and disseminating it to future generations. Only the alert, conscious and morally strong can manage to remain in the lead, not the casual, reticent and unconcerned.

Vice-Chancellors, directors, and chairpersons of universities, institutions and organisations were considered to be the embodiments of leading lives that had internalised moral, ethical, and humanistic values. They were seen as the creators and disseminators of knowledge, with the highest levels of integrity, devotion, and commitment to their profession. Things have changed drastically from when around 20 universities in India could record stellar achievements in hitting the 800-mark over seven decades. We need expansion and more institutions of higher and professional learning. But it is the basic principle of planning and management that when systems expand rapidly, special attention must be paid to prevent the dilution of output quality and work culture. This did not happen in India. The Central and state governments pressurised universities to generate their own resources.

This led to the opening of B.Ed. and correspondence courses in a large number of universities, with due approval of the University Grants Commission (UGC). Everyone knew that these were meant to generate resources for the universities, augment their infrastructure, open other courses, and launch new programmes.

Unfortunately, it was also the beginning of the open exploitation of students and made a lasting impact on the work culture of universities. Wherever there were chances of 'extra resources', politicians would step in! At that stage, political interference began in the appointment of 'pliable' VCs. Several of those who were a bit out-of-date suffered on various counts. This was when several VCs were found wanting in people's expectations, who became convinced that these VCs and heads of institutions had reached their coveted positions only because of their personality traits other than 'merit and academic excellence'. Again, exceptions apart, it is tough to visualise large-scale enhancement in the institutions of credibility and acceptability if the leadership is weak, if the autonomy stands compromised, and if academics are made subservient to bureaucrats!

Banaras Hindu University (BHU) offered a great learning experience to educational planners, innovators, and entrepreneurs. Pandit Madan Mohan Malaviya had a vision; he persuaded the best among educationists from all over India to join the new university 'for a cause'! He invited Dr Sarvepalli Radhakrishnan to become the VC. Pandit Malaviya inspired young and old alike, exhorting them to move ahead on the path of discovering new knowledge, disseminating it, and utilising it for the welfare of the weak, deprived, and downtrodden. It is such intellectual leadership and professional autonomy supported by sincere effort and great spirit that can transform institutions as well as the entire higher education scenario.

Chapter 4

Higher Education: Vision, Growth, and Governance

The Background of a Rich Heritage

The traditional Indian *Gurukula* model from ancient India was unique, and did not require any formalised rule-based regulatory system of governance from outside. Each Gurukula or ancient educational institute was fully autonomous and was supported in trust and faith by the society and the rulers, it served. Much could be learnt from the ancient Indian tradition of the knowledge quest, transfer, and utilisation so much so that great institutions like Nalanda, Taxila, Vikramshila and others continue to be unique exemplars of our country's history of education systems.

Even today, top-level international universities have reached the credibility they enjoy solely because of autonomy, and total absence from outside interference and control. Inevitably, there were constraints in the implementation of such practices in situations when the State provided public funds and was duty-bound to ensure its appropriate usage and accountability. The trust deficit of pre-Independence days perpetuates even now, and similar patterns of overseeing accountability persist.

From Social Support to State Control

Several notable initiatives can be recalled from the country's pre-Independence days that ignited afresh the quest for knowledge that had permeated Indian society at practically every level from the times of the *Gurukula*, led by learned and wise men and women. Opening educational institutions was considered a pious task, one of the notable means to repay the 'Rishi Rin', debt to learned knowledge creators. Support came from within societies, especially the affluent and the rulers of that time. Those were the golden days of a unique level of mutual trust and respect. Any interference from any quarters was unimaginable.

Before Independence from British rule, outstanding initiatives were launched in this country in higher education, purely with help from philanthropists. The Banaras Hindu University (BHU) is the primary example of the vision of Pandit Madan Mohan Malaviya, who lived a life fully devoted to Vedic principles and practices, and advocated equal respect for all religions; and had deep faith in the concept of 'unity in diversity' that traditionally abounded in India. But he had the vision and knew how relevant it would be to acquire new knowledge, and how it could be harmonised with the great wisdom of ancient India. His university gave equal importance to the study of the Vedas, as also to establishing the first modern college of engineering.

The establishment of the Aligarh Muslim University, Baroda University, and Mysore University were also very significant developments. There emerged a large list of colleges as well.

Post-Independence Growth in Education

In post-Independent India, in the early 1950s, there were just about thirty universities or Higher Education Institutions (HEI) and 695 colleges all over India. The literacy rates were around 18-20 per cent, and access to education was severely restricted at every stage. There was a very inspiring inheritance of the freedom struggle: No other struggle for freedom had focused so much on education as had been emphasised by the Indian leaders of the pre-Independence period!

Mahatma Gandhi saw education as the 'ray of hope' for the deprived and the way to bring them hope after several generations. For decades, he had worked dexterously on his model of basic education, *Buniyadi Talim*. He had a very clear vision of the shape of higher education in Independent India. He had delivered a historic speech at the foundation day ceremony of BHU on 4 February 1916. By 1947, this university had created a distinguished place for itself among Indian universities, primarily because of the model of governance it developed under the nationalistic fervour and universal vision of Pandit Madan Mohan Malaviya, which was subsequently strengthened by the presence of distinguished scholars and academic stalwarts of the stature of Dr Sarvepalli Radhakrishnan. At the time of Independence, universities of Allahabad, Patna, Madras, Calcutta, AMU, and Shanti Niketan had a very respectful international presence among distinguished centres of learning and knowledge. India had a reputed scholar as its first education minister, Maulana Abul Kalam Azad, and internationally known scientists and scholars, including C V Raman, Homi J Bhabha, S S Bhatnagar, S N Bose, D S Kothari, Ramaswami Mudaliyar among others.

(The list of colleges included affiliated colleges, university colleges, constituent colleges, PG Centres, off-campus Centres and recognised Centres.)

In spite of severe resource constraints, with the futuristic vision and foresight of the academic community and political leadership, India went ahead with innovative plans and programmes for expanding higher education, setting up new institutions in relevant areas, particularly for the advancement of science and technology. This led to establishing great centres for nuclear science and space research, now known internationally as Tata Institute of Fundamental Research (TIFR), Bhabha Atomic Research Centre (BARC), and Indian Space Research Organisation (ISRO). Further, the Council of Scientific and Industrial Research (CSIR), National Physical Laboratory (NPL), several new universities, and several specialised laboratories in specific areas of research, innovation, and applications of the outcomes initiated considerable advances and helped to create a rich pool of young scholars and scientists. Addressing the convocation of Allahabad University, Pandit Jawaharlal Nehru put his perception on higher education in these words:

> A university stands for humanism, for tolerance, for reason, for adventure of ideas and for the search of truth. It stands for the onward march of the human race towards even higher objectives. If the universities discharge their duties adequately, then it is all well with the nation and the people. (Kothari, 2000: 108).

On another occasion, he exhorted young people to test their mettle and contribute to building a new India:

> Every generation has to fight anew the battle for freedom. Otherwise, we grow soft and forget the basic values of life and freedom and tend to lose their essence. Now a chance comes to all of us and, more especially to the young to test their mettle and their patriotism. Let this challenge be considered an opportunity and be met with strength, dignity, discipline and fortitude, so that out of this trial a new and better India might be fashioned by the efforts and sacrifices of her children. (Ibid.: 32).

In consonance with the spirit of the Constitution of India, in spite of severe constraints thrust upon national resources, independent India remained steadfastly committed to provide equal opportunity to all in school education, and to the willing, inclined, and talented in higher education. The national vision was best comprehended in the words of Dr Sarvepalli Radhakrishnan, who, ever conscious of universal access, quality, and excellence made this universally encouraging and acceptable statement: 'Education is a universal right, and not a class privilege.' Further, he said, 'Intellectual work is not for all, it is only for the intellectually competent.' (Radhakrishnan, 1990: 509-513). No matter what changes may have occurred in individual aspirations and national expectations from the universities and institutions of higher learning, the following summarisation by the teacher-philosopher-statesman not only comprehensively unveils the role of universities, but also lays down candidly the role of teachers:

> 'If our universities, which showed so much promise on the eve of Independence, now appear to be in a state of disarray, it is because they have been increasingly invaded by masses of people who have no regard for intellectual

competence or aptitude for academic work. We have made short work of tests of intellectual competence in order to make peace with every kind of social and political pressure.' (Ibid.)

The Turbulent Trajectory of the Education System

Back in 2017, Pankaj Chandra prudently analyses how the governments entered into the managements of educational institutions, and the rest, as they say, is history:

> The nineteenth and early twentieth centuries, when many of these colleges were being established, remain the golden period for private support of higher education in India. Sometime in the 1950s, the government decided to support these institutions with significant operating grants, thus starting an era of State control in academic institutions. The control of these grant-in-aid institutions passed from nimble, engaged donors to stodgy, suspecting government bureaucrats.

The HEIs saw in the government, a source of easy financial aid that would otherwise have been unavailable to them. The government, in turn, argued that since it was providing financial support to universities, it should have a say in their decision-making processes. It wanted to influence the appointment of these institution's leadership and, subsequently, have a say in the selection of its faculty. The government insidiously imposed its own rules and regulations on the university, displacing the governance system that was already in existence (which, it can be argued, was less transparent, but was decisive and focused). The Central Government started propagating its own educational vision by establishing largely standalone central institutions that focused on specific disciplines or provided training for a single profession. Undergraduates were, therefore, deprived of a well-grounded, holistic education. By the early 1960s, the foundation of *Sarkarikaran* was in place. Gradually, the control of the establishment grew both in institutions established by the Union government, and State governments just followed suit.

During the Emergency in 1975-77, with complete government control, intellectual endeavour was undermined in all walks of society. In the 1980s, State governments competed with each other to lower the eligibility standards not only for entry to professional colleges, but also sanctioned HEIs without arranging for necessary resources. How they impacted the quality in higher education is best illustrated by a reference to the massive growth of professional institutions, offering teacher-education qualifications as outlined in the Ministry of Human Resource Development (MHRD), NEP-2020, para 15.2:

> According to the Justice J.S. Verma Committee (2012) constituted by the Supreme Court, a majority of stand-alone TEIs, over 10,000 in number, are not even attempting serious teacher education but are essentially selling degrees for a price. Regulatory effort has, so far, neither been able to curb the malpractices in the system, nor enforce basic standards for quality, and in fact have had the negative effect of curbing the growth of excellence and innovations in the sector. The sector and its regulatory systems are therefore in urgent need of revitalisation through radical action in order to raise standards and restore integrity, credibility, efficacy and high quality to the teacher education system.

Current State of Disarray

The state of disarray, which was a matter of concern over seven decades ago, has become far more complex at this juncture. The immense expansion in HEIs and enrolments could be one contributing factor. To correct the situation, the first challenge is to keep the quality of education in the HEIs suitably advanced to meet internationally acceptable levels, apart from meeting national needs and requirements. The systems of governance, management, and administrations have undergone considerable changes in response to new challenges. These need to be scrutinised and examined in view of the pace of change that has been unexpectedly accelerated during this century. Presently, we are seriously deficient in efforts to ensure quality and excellence in several of the HEIs. India needs sound academic leadership, and a dynamic system of governance and its structures.

Here are some critical questions posed to the system of governance:

- How and why did India, while expanding its higher education system (HES), allow the dilution of basic expectations of quality, excellence, creation, and utilisation of new knowledge from universities and specialised HEIs?
- Did the leadership lack dynamism, commitment, and inspiration?
- Was there an inadequacy of necessary human and fiscal inputs?

The On-going Challenge

We are now in the third decade of this century and it is high time that we comprehend that 'The industrial revolution has bequeathed us the production line theory of education.' (Harari,

2018: 309). The pertinent questions that we need to address are:
- Is higher education now only meant to prepare young people for jobs?
- Isn't such an approach injurious to personality development and search for truth?
- Is the universally accepted ideal of education to promote the liberty of mind and freedom of thought too tough to sustain?
- Have we adhered to traditional pedagogies for far too long?

The traditional classroom-teacher-taught model that was globally prevalent, stood seriously challenged during the mid-twentieth century. We persisted with it for far too long. As the pace of change accelerates, it requires corresponding changes in policies, focus on student choices and interests, new pedagogies, and more prominently than the past, in systems of governance, administration and management.

The Covid-19 pandemic posed new challenges to practically every aspect of higher education. This encompassed the very approach to new pedagogies, course content, and respect for individual choices of the learner! It necessitated serious transformation in the structure and approach of governance and management.

In a federal setup of degrees, grades and credits, the issues of equivalence, transfers from one system to another, and the need for institutional networking that helps maintain global standards, just cannot be ignored. Hence a coordination mechanism at the Central and State level is necessary. Over the last seven decades, large-scale expansion was inevitable, and it did take place. However, corresponding structural changes in management and governance could not keep pace with the emerging demands.

The inadequacy of such changes has been adequately reflected in the National Education Policy, NEP-2020. Dynamic systems of governance that aim at assisting the academia in quality, excellence, and new knowledge can gain a lot from the manner in which well-known international institutions are functioning, creating new knowledge, experimenting with new management systems, and utilising Information and Communication Technology (ICT) to augment their effort. In fact, every institution requires an innovative leadership and its own system of governance that suits the personality of the university/institution. Academic leaders must learn from others but be his 'own person' when it comes to implementation.

Preparing for the Emerging Scenario

Universities and HEIs in India could also be categorised on the basis of the source of funding and resource generation. Funding comes from the Central Government, State Governments, and self-financing initiatives within State-funded universities. India now has several private universities, colleges, and other degree-awarding institutions. The most sought-after universities of national importance like the Indian Institutes of Technology (IITs), Indian Institutes of Management (IIMs), and the All-India Institute of Medical Sciences (AIIMS), are fully funded by the Central Government.

The Structure: The President of India is the Visitor of Central universities, and the Governor of a state is the Chancellor of State-funded universities. Private universities have other arrangements for the post of Chancellor. The Executive Council, Board of Management, and Governors constitute the top body. The Vice-Chancellor (VC) is supposed to implement its decisions and instructions. The VCs are appointed for a fixed duration of five years (in some states, it is three years) by a search-cum-selection committee constituted by the Visitor and/or Chancellor. It submits a panel of three or five names, out of which one is picked as the VC. The VC is supposed to be a scholar of eminence, and must embody values and ethics, and be known for his or her compassion, vision and empathy, and be committed to create and generate new knowledge. The VC is the academic leader and the university is expected to stand behind him or her in implementing ideas and achieving them as well as meeting the national goals set up by the education policy at the national level. The Central Advisory Board of Education (CABE) is the top national body to advise the government in all matters of education, and that includes structural changes and also uplifting of the systems of governance.

The point to be noted in the context of governance is terrifying, to say the least. Although the former Chief Justice of India highlighted the horrible state of affairs in 2012, it had to be repeated in 2020! Obviously not much had been achieved in these intervening eight years! The story is quite similar in medical, engineering, management, and other sought-after professional courses. Commercialisation of education is a daunting issue in India at every level. Our systems of coaching, particularly some few popular coaching systems have intruded deep within institutions, disturbing and destroying the accepted pedagogies that are supposed to kindle ideas and imagination among children. More often than not, papers are regularly leaked in entrance and competitive exams. This, however, can be tackled. It requires leadership qualities and support from decision makers at every level. Everyone is expected to adhere to honesty and transparency, irrespective of ideological or political commitments.

National Education Policy

India's first comprehensive national education policy came in 1968, followed by more policies in 1986 and 1992, and the latest, National Policy on Education, NEP-2020, is under active implementation at present. Each of these appreciated the role and importance of upgrading the systems of educational administration and management in accordance with the goals and objectives articulated. The NEP-2020 (p. 4) mentions:

> The aim of education in ancient India was not just the acquisition of knowledge as a preparation for life in this world, or life beyond schooling, but for the complete realisation and liberation of the soul. World class institutions in India such as Takshashila, Nalanda, Vikramshila, Vallabhi, set the highest standards of multidisciplinary teaching and research and hosted scholars and students from across backgrounds and countries.

The extent of successful implementation depends on the strength and dynamism acquired by the system of governance and its manner of prioritising the initiatives expected to be launched to fulfil the aims and goals stated in the policy document. A thorough transformation has become necessary after two years of the pandemic, which disturbed education systems unexpectedly around the globe. Academic leadership was put through unprecedented testing in handling this unforeseen situation.

Academic Leadership

Common people have to deal with government functionaries at various levels. The upper levels of the bureaucratic hierarchy, in various areas and departments, have visible and experiential commonalities. Seniors expect respect, are conscious of their position and power, and are always keen to punish those who commit a wrong, evoking the fear of authority while dealing with those whom they are supposed to serve. Invariably, they refer to past precedents and are generally not interested in taking risks and launching innovations. This approach just does not work when it comes to academia. Societies that do not offer adequate respect to their teachers rarely flourish. Those who become part of educational systems within institutions and also in government and its departments must clearly appreciate and internalise the difference between the bureaucratic approach and the academic approach (Rajput 2001: 238-249).

It has been observed that when academics, scholars, or researchers assume charge of a leadership position as VC, chairperson, or director of a distinguished public university or professional organisation devoted to research and development, they are invariably, overwhelmed by administrative and bureaucratic procedures and stipulations. All of a sudden, they are steeped into its complex administrative and financial workings and management. Those who really appreciate the difference between academic and bureaucratic administration are able to successfully delegate most of the general administration responsibilities to registrars and financial advisors.

Persons in leadership positions will command respect for their contribution to knowledge creation and research, and ultimately contribute to the academic life of the nation (*ibid.* 247-248). They must continue to be focused on their academics, despite new responsibilities, and continue working on innovations in their areas of specialisation, while also managing people and their institutions. The leaders need not focus on an individual lapse but skilfully explore the factors responsible for any individuals not being able to realise their full potential and capability. Academic heads must always participate actively in serious professional discussions and treat institution management as an art, not a craft. They must continuously interact with colleagues with due deference, and acknowledge their contribution in realising the objectives, goals, and vision envisaged in the initial stages of the establishment of the institution, and any alterations that might be necessary in a dynamic scenario in the field concerned. They should be ready to face all challenges and manage conflict situations.

In the present decade, one of the most significant objectives of education and learning as identified by UNESCO and accepted globally is, 'learning to live together' along with learning to know, learning to do, and learning to be. This defines the horizon opening up when new age academic leaders assume charge as institutional heads.

Percept to Practice

Impediments to improvements in higher education are really a cause of concern (Rajput 2022). One of these is the inadequacy of resources, both in the workforce and in materials. If funds for research and innovations are scarce, and universities suffer from 40-60 per cent academic staff vacancies, then, this in itself is a bleak scenario. There is one more serious issue which is often swept under the carpet. Apart from these problems, we must also ponder over the external influences that make or mar the decision-making skills of our academic leaders. In ancient Indian tradition, even kings and emperors would never have thought of imposing their persons of interest as chiefs of Nalanda, Vikramshila or Vallabhi! Politicians would rather believe that all talk about university autonomy and its being headed by an outstanding individual is, 'meant only for academic discussions and nothing more'. They are worried about the recommendations in the NEP-2020—which propose constituting a strong Board of Governors (BoG), that shall become the appointing authority of VCs and other heads of HEIs. The NEP-2020 clearly mentions: 'It is envisaged that all HEIs will be incentivised, supported and mentored during this process, and shall aim to become autonomous and have such an empowered BoG by 2035.'

The Kerala and Tamil Nadu Governments are said to be working on independent education policies, having rejected the NEP-2020. If this really happens, it will permanently damage the interests of the young persons from these two states, on both the national and international stage. The current systems of governance cannot be expected to deliver either in terms of excellence or a sound work culture under such circumstances.

A Case for Case Studies

In a slightly different context, one can study the case of the National Council for Teacher Education (NCTE) created by an Act of Parliament in 1993. There was a long-standing demand for this from senior and sincere teacher-educators for over two decades. The NCTE became operational in 1995-96, and within the next three years, made its presence felt throughout the country, particularly among all those interested in education and teacher education. It followed the policy of being 'supportive yet firm' and it really worked. Once convinced that every institution had been made fully aware of the basic minimum inputs required both for the workforce and materials required in Teacher Education Institutions (TEIs), it implemented these firmly. On one occasion, a State government sanctioned seventy-odd TEIs to function with immediate effect, without caring for NCTE stipulations. The NCTE, after making sincere yet unsuccessful efforts to convince the State authorities to put a stop to this, then had to issue notices in the media indicating that the degrees earned through these institutions would not be recognised. This approach worked and the State authorities had to withdraw the sanctions.

In another instance, a State Open University invited applications for admission to B Ed correspondences courses, again flouting the NCTE stipulations, prompting the NCTE to issue public notices about it being unrecognised. It worked again. The credibility of the organisation was not only established, but it was also appreciated for its tough stand.

It is also relevant to mention that NCTE, which arrived on the scene as a trailblazer created positive vibes in academia, and received appreciation even from the perpetual critics of every innovative initiative. Unfortunately, it squandered away its credibility and acceptability within no time. It is for serious researchers and scholars in education, management, and governance to research about this organisation, and many others, on how the initial credibility was established, and what led to its sharp decline.

By 2012, the Justice Verma Committee had to make these shocking remarks: 'A majority of stand-alone TEIs—over 10,000 in number are not even attempting serious teacher education but are essentially selling degrees for a price.' A study of these examples can help identify indicators that create both positivity and negativity, and the impact on the growth and development of academic institutions. The appropriate research will also reveal what is needed to be achieved in the years ahead to ensure institutional functioning at an optimum level.

The Task Ahead

India is moving ahead with educational plans and programmes that are future-oriented, and inspiring to the generations ahead. It is the *Kulapati*, the VC, who would be responsible for creating a learning environment rich enough to lead the disciple from humanity to divinity (Rajput, 2016: 90-91). The Shanti Parva of the Mahabharata highlights the responsibility of the guru in pragmatic terms: *Gurur Gurutamodhamah*; the guru-teacher or mentor, can transform the learner from a person to a personality, even guiding him on the path from humanity to divinity. It requires an ambience that encourages purity of thought, speech, and action. It may appear tough at this stage, but India has achieved it in the past. It can do so again in spite of the hurdles, deficits, and deficiencies at present. In spite of impediments being thrown in the well-initiated implementation of the recent transformational resolves, the nation must move ahead on the policy mandate (MHRD, NEP-2020: 19.2), which states:

> It is effective governance and leadership that enables the creation of a culture of excellence and innovation in higher education institutions. The common feature of all world-class institutions globally including India has indeed been the existence of strong self-governance and

outstanding merit-based appointment of institutional leaders.

In this day and age, no nation can afford to ignore what was anticipated by several luminaries at the time of the decimation of the era of imperialism that 'future empires shall be empires of knowledge'. These are the days of knowledge power and knowledge economy. It is encouraging that the Indian academia and scholarship accepts the new outlook, and this finds reflection in the resolve made at the national level (*ibid.*: 19.4):

> All leadership positions and Heads of institutions shall be offered to persons with high academic qualifications and demonstrated administrative and leadership capabilities along with abilities to manage complex situations. Leaders of an HEI will demonstrate strong alignment to constitutional values and the overall vision of an institution, along with attributes such as a strong social commitment, belief in teamwork, pluralism, ability to work with diverse people, and a positive outlook. The selection shall be carried out by the BOG through a rigorous, impartial, merit-based, and competency-based process by an Eminent Expert Committee constituted by the BOG.

It is a very encouraging and inspiring blueprint for moving towards excellence in the national knowledge quest, its creation, assimilation, and utilisation in human welfare. Working under tough conditions, Indian universities must remain conscious of the adage attributed to Napoleon: 'Men are powerless against the future; institutions alone fix the destinies of nations.' India's history, heritage, and tradition clearly indicate how institutions have played a sustained role in maintaining the continuity, simultaneously accepting noble thoughts from all around. India is bound to regain its legitimate position in the comity of nations as long as its higher education institutions prepare disciplined young persons of exemplary character, courage, commitment to values and ethics in life.

Chapter 5

Transformative Education and Education Policies

The earlier national policies on education of 1968, 1986, and 1992 made sincere attempts to bring in reforms in curricula, pedagogy, and the system for assessments and examinations, but the craze for higher marks, and English medium schools, discounted all such efforts. Mahatma Gandhi's understanding of India, and the mind of the Indian people was unparalleled; he knew the necessity of acquiring skills, working with hands, health, nutrition, and acquisition of character coupled with the internalisation of moral, ethical, humanistic, and constitutional values. And this would be achieved only when the goal of education is man-making, character development, and transforming youngsters into fully-blossomed personality.

This is the eternal challenge before education, and the implementers of any education policy must seriously examine the continuity of the epistemological basis— and practical realities right from reinforcing the *Buniyadi Talim* and yet meeting the challenges before them. They have before them a policy that is, 'rooted to culture and committed to progress'.

The Emerging Indian Education System — NEP 2020

The eagerly awaited New Education Policy, released in 2020 (MHRD, NEP-2020), was welcomed enthusiastically. The NEP-2020 addresses both national needs as well as meets the requirements of the international scenario. It has all the ingredients that can pave the way for a truly transformed India. An incisive scrutiny indicates how essential it is to nurture human beings imbued with character, commitment, and concern. The Policy acknowledges the guiding light it derived from the, 'Rich heritage of ancient and eternal Indian knowledge and thought.'

The pursuit of knowledge, wisdom and truth are the highest goals of human life. The NEP-2020 acknowledges that education in ancient India did not just prepare you for life in this world but also took care of the realisation and liberation of the individual soul.

The ancient Indian system of education valued the pursuit of knowledge with the sole objective of utilising it for the welfare of humanity. Can there be better comprehension of the essential unity of human beings as one family? And in a family, differences and diversities are accepted and respected. This is what the NEP-2020 has subsumed in words and spirit. It recalls how the ancient Indian education system strove tirelessly to make seminal contributions in diverse fields of knowledge including mathematics, astronomy, metallurgy, surgery, health concerns, architecture, engineering, ship building, navigation, yoga, fine arts, and much more. These are the gems of knowledge that luminaries such as Charak, Susruta, Aryabhata, Bhaskaracharya, Brahmagupta, Nagarjuna, Gautama, Maitreyi, Gargi, Thiruvalluvur, and so many more, left for generations to follow.

Every Indian student, as an inheritor of this great legacy, must be made familiar with it and accept the responsibility to enhance it further through excellence in the chosen area of activity and expertise. It paves the way to move out of the clutches of a transplanted system that prompts over eight lakh children annually to go abroad for further studies! The competence, commitment, and ingenuity displayed at the implementation stage can once again make India a globally sought-after educational hub in the foreseeable future.

Undoubtedly, as already mentioned, young Indians have established their credibility overseas, right from being employed by NASA to obtaining jobs in Silicon Valley. But the lowering of the standards of learner attainments in Indian education across the spectrum has certainly dented global credibility. Apart from national concerns that are well-known, NEP 2020 also has to gel appropriately with global concerns and initiatives that are being pursued via international collaboration. An issue of paramount importance is the wanton exploitation of natural resources, leading to irreversible damage to the sensitive man-nature bond.

It is easy to locate elements in NEP-2020 that lead to the Sarvodya that Gandhiji had learnt while in South Africa that prominently highlights equity, equality, working with hands, and value nurturance from the beginning of schooling. Once curriculum designers, textbook writers and textual material developers are well-versed in the philosophy behind the formulation of *Buniyadi Talim* and its relevance to India and its people, they would really be able to create a generation proud of its history, culture, and heritage. All of it appears very prominently in the policy that, envisions an education system rooted to the Indian ethos that contributes directly to transforming India.

Universal education was considered the ray of hope for one and all and NEP-2020 endorses it as, 'The basic right of every child.' It must be correctly interpreted as the right of the child to get support in drawing the best out of the body, mind and spirit. It is the child's right to make choices of learning areas according to personal likings and interests. It would be violating a child's personal territory if subjected to a regimen that impedes the child's, 'power of ideas and power of imagination.' This is what the present examination system has been reduced to. The policy envisages drastic transformation in this crucial area. The recommendations on 'Holistic and multidisciplinary education' will permit free flow of fresh air in schools and HEIs. It could lead to a surge of curiosity and creativity, among young minds! That is the need of the current time, and of the future. Now onwards, in knowledge societies, progress would depend on the quality of manpower, and the measure of entrepreneurial skills and on the level of innovative contributions. Our education system needs to make educationists well-versed with specific national needs to bring the 'last man in the line,' in the centrality of thought and action. Policy makers must understand the import of the one per cent lucky individuals owning 73 per cent of the wealth of the country, and that this just cannot be an example of an evenly balanced strategy of growth and development!

Transformational Reforms

We have a great opportunity of introducing new or revised transformational reforms in education at this juncture. These are defining years in Indian education reforms, resplendent with high expectations, generational, aspirational and inevitable transformational initiatives. NEP-2020 is already in the process of implementation. It has the strength of unprecedented high levels of consultations on the one hand, and a rare outcome of two successive committee reports. The first committee, tasked to prepare the draft of NEP-2020, was appointed by MHRD in October 2015 under the chairmanship of T S R Subramanian. The committee submitted its report in April 2016.

The MHRD felt the need for more consultations and appointed another committee under Dr K Kasturirangan as chairman. This report, submitted in end-May 2019, was made public on the same day, and everyone was invited to offer comments and observations. The Kasturirangan Committee took conscious note of the inadequate presence of the education of the heart and hand. Two of its suggestions were path-breaking. It recommended complete abolition of the bifurcation of liberal and vocational education. The report and the suggestions were examined in depth by experts in concerned professional institutions and the MHRD. The suggestions received from individuals, experts, scholars, institutions, and the outcomes of numerous consultation meetings and interactions constituted a rare collection of documents and data which were analysed through well-organised researches and studies and these are now presenting the social, cultural and economic connections of education to the swift changes that engulf the entire content and process of education in our schools and institutions of higher learning and research.

Several unprecedented challenges have emerged for educational policy planners and implementers.

The need to accept and adopt a holistic approach to education instead of focusing only on the education of the head has been highlighted in NEP-2020. Holistic education requires serious conceptual and structural changes in the content and process of education. It is necessary to realise the scientific basis of the importance of learning in the early years. It has been acknowledged that 0-8 are the most crucial and formative years, and this realisation comes forth very strongly in NEP-2020 when it recommends substantial changes in school education in the format of 5+3+3+4. These represent foundational stage of grades 1-2, preparatory stage of grades 3-5, middle stage covering grades 6-8 and secondary stage of four years, 9-12. It recommends changes in the RTE Act of 2009 to include all children in the age group 3 to 18.

Accepting this suggestion of focusing on the early years and removing the distinction between liberal and vocational education will usher in an era of much-needed focus on education of the heart. The preamble of NEP-2020, that was shared by the MHRD for public consultation, mentioned that it should also be properly comprehended at the implementation stage that education must assist not only in developing cognitive skills— both 'foundational skills' of literacy and numeracy and 'higher-order' cognitive skills such as critical thinking and problem-solving skills—but also social and emotional skills, also referred to as 'soft skills', including cultural awareness and empathy, perseverance and grit, teamwork and leadership, among others. The process by which children and adults acquire these competencies is also referred to as Social and Emotional Learning (SEL).

Global Context of the National Education Policy

Policies are formulated on the strong foundation of the outcomes of an incisive analysis of past experiences, coupled with a futuristic vision that could respond to emerging issues, concerns and aspirations.

Once the NEP-2020 is appropriately implemented, every learner will undoubtedly be exposed to modern knowledge imparted by way of education at institutions following the most modern pedagogy, with due emphasis on critical thinking, creativity, and innovations, aimed at developing the full human potential. The NEP-2020 acknowledges that higher education, must aim to develop good, thoughtful, well-rounded, and creative individuals. Obviously, early school education would take cognisance of these aspects in the most sensitive years.

Several of the initiatives and steps included in the NEP-2020, when implemented in letter and spirit, can transform India into an international education hub. Recommendations on multidisciplinary universities, robust autonomy, revamping of curriculum and pedagogy, reforms in the governance of HEIs, the creation of the National Research Foundation (NRF), and of the National Educational Technology Forum (NETF), are the positive additions towards enhancing the quality and contemporary relevance of the Indian education system. These would certainly attract the attention of corresponding international institutions and organisations.

To attract students from overseas: Young persons from all over the globe are interested in understanding India. The availability of internationally relevant curricula in the history, heritage and culture of India, as also the modern subject areas could attract enough foreign students, helping us to achieve the goal of 'internationalisation at home'. Some well thought-out suggestions like opening foreign campuses by established Indian institutions and permitting top international universities to operate in India would effectively put Indian education firmly on the International podium, with dignity and credibility. Shared courses of studies with reputed international institutions could pave the way for much-needed morale boosting and would ignite the competitive, yet healthy, desire to excel.

One has to be cautious on certain aspects. Global credibility and recognition would require certain amount of revamping and improving levels of infrastructure and facilities. The NEP-2020 assures this, and states that 'Every classroom shall have access to the latest educational technology that enables better learning experiences.'

Teacher-student ratio: There can be no compromise on the professionally accepted figure for teacher-taught ratio. This raises several related requirements. Quality cannot be raised by merely engaging guest teachers, teachers on lecture-based payments, para-or contract teachers, and at the same time keeping countless posts of school-teachers vacant! In HEIs, the quality of products, research, and innovations will be greatly impeded if there are 40-60 per cent vacant academic positions! The NEP-2020 boldly acknowledges this concern:

> The teacher must be at the Centre of the fundamental reforms in the education system. The new education policy must help re-establish teachers, at all levels, as the most respected and essential members of our society, because they truly shape our next generation of citizens. It must do everything to empower teachers and help them do their job as effectively as possible.

Expressing serious concern on the quality of teacher education, it is recommended that by 2030, all of the present one-year school-teacher preparation programmes will be replaced by four-year integrated teacher-education programmes. The four-year integrated teacher preparation programmes had been initiated in the four institutions of the NCERT in 1964 and the teachers who qualified were indeed far ahead of others in their professional performance in schools and in teacher-education institutions. Unfortunately, this scheme was not replicated or continued. In higher education, the education policy acknowledges the 'criticality, quality and engagement' of the faculty. It also accepts that the motivation of faculty in terms of teaching, research, and service in HEIs is far lower than the desired level.

Several steps have been listed to attract the best, motivated, and capable faculty in HEIs. These include:
- Correct teacher-student ratio
- Unhindered access to education technology
- Freedom to design preferred curricular and pedagogical approaches
- Incentives such as appropriate rewards, promotions, recognitions, and moving into institutional leadership, as per qualifications

Syllabus Reduction

The 2018 announcement on reducing the 'NCERT curriculum by half' indicates a much sought after and well-considered response from the HRD Minister. His courageous statement of reducing the curriculum load can have far-reaching consequences for the future of the education system. It has the strength of futuristic professional vision and extraordinary courage on the part of decision makers. Could it really happen? People, including parents and children, are keen and curious to know whether it would really take practical shape. And if it indeed materialises in word and spirit, it would be an outstanding educational reform that would change the approach to the process of teaching and learning, open up new vistas for personality development and talent nurturing in Indian schools, which are busy with educating 230 million children!

We would like to envision a drastic change in the school environment, children rushing to schools, working in groups, performing experiments, participating in sports and games, and above all, being free from the fear of examinations! Implemented in true word and spirit, it could really usher in a revolutionary change in the life of young children and adolescents, the future generations of India. The present situation, encompassing excessive curriculum load, huge weighty school bags, rote learning, fear of the future, neglect of the mother tongue, especially in the initial stages, focus only on the Board Examinations, marks/grades, and a couple of related factors, impedes the blossoming of the instinctive bounty of curiosity, creativity, and the 'power' of ideas and of imagination. The change envisaged could bring childhood back to children in schools, which indeed is their right. The stark reality is that education systems the world over are known to be most change-resistant. Voices from vested interest and unaware 'experts' are already audible that reducing syllabi or making textbooks thinner would reduce learning!

In 1989, illustrious author R K Narayan, and member Rajya Sabha, said in his maiden speech:

> More children on account of this daily burden develop a stoop and hang their arms forward like a chimpanzee while walking.... It is a cruel harsh life imposed on her and I present her case before this House and the

Honourable members to think over and devise a remedy by changing the whole educational system and outlook so that childhood has a chance to bloom.

Emphasising that an average child carried bags strapped to his back like a 'pack-mule', he said:
The hardship starts right at home when straight from bed the child is pulled out and got ready for school even before his faculties are awake. He or she is groomed and stuffed into a uniform and packed off with a loaded bag on his/her back.

His speech attracted nationwide debate on the urgency to initiate remedial action and was persistently emphasised by all concerned. Consequently, in March 1992, the Union government appointed a national advisory committee under the chairmanship of Professor Yash Pal with the aim of advising on the ways and means to reduce the load on school students at all levels, particularly the young students, while improving quality of learning including capability for lifelong self-learning skill formulation.

It was also indicated that the committee would examine all aspects related to curricula, entrance criteria, and exit attainments at various levels and also look at the stress caused by the fear of examinations.

The committee, in consultation with experts and stakeholders, delineated factors that needed to be remedied. These included looking at:
- Imparting information instead of knowledge
- Involving experts not familiar with classroom situations in curriculum development and textbook writing
- Updating archaic teaching approaches

- Centralising the curriculum
- Studying the nature of the examination pattern

Practically every education-conscious nation changes its school curriculum every five years, if not earlier. Provision is also kept for including a Frontline Curriculum even earlier, before the next curriculum changes so as to accommodate, without delay, new aspects that must be brought within the learning ambit of children. India continues with its school curriculum framework prepared in 2005, which, to say the least, is indeed puzzling!

Textbook Load: In the public's perception, heavy textbooks and load of the school bag is the creation of the national advisory body on education, the NCERT. This, in real terms, can only be partially true. The simple recommendation that there should be no school bags and no homework for children in classes I and II appears very reasonable and pedagogically sound. Its implementation cannot be a problem. But how many schools in the country have even made a sincere attempt to try it out? On the other hand, a majority of the private schools that follow the CBSE syllabus and use NCERT books, invariably include additional books and other materials from private publishers. We cannot close our eyes to these so-called 'economic and dividend-oriented' practices that are now widespread in a significant number of schools. These books are sold at exorbitant prices, often within the school premises.

How then, can one expect such managements to focus on creating a value-based learning environment conducive to joyful learning?

The gradual loss of credibility and public acceptance of government-run schools has led to several unacceptable practices in the much sought after private schools. These invariably accentuate avoidable stress and burden on the learners, which is naturally faced by parents and families. When readymade projects are available in school bookshops at a price, who takes the blame for the resulting loss of a child's real-time and hands-on learning, personal initiative and acquisition of skills? Our systems have become so lethargic that schools do not even modify their timetable judiciously to avoid daily loading of bags with, textbooks, and exercise books of all subjects! More often than not, the stress and strain are also accentuated because of professionally underprepared teachers, and the nonavailability of qualified guidance counsellors. Parental pressure on obtaining more and more marks is an additional issue.

Challenges for the Future: The current education system faces a daunting challenge, as its immediate implication is the rewriting of textbooks. Every state government has come on board, convinced that the decision is in the best interest of every learner. The new system is expected to help in developing the child's total personality, inculcate self-confidence, and nurture the inherent curiosity and creativity that under our current excessive syllabus and memory-based examination system is invariably crushed. The powers of ideas and imagination are lost in the fear of examinations and the pressure to secure 'extra marks'.

The system requires an attitudinal transformation on the part of both teachers and parents to let examinations become an adventurous challenge instead of a fearsome Damocles' sword! An intensive programme is needed for making state-and district/block-level functionaries accept and acknowledge the merits of a reduced syllabus. The children will enjoy the additional time and space they can now use for diverse activities that will help them grow mentally, physically, and socially, and become creative and constructive members of society.

Revising Textbooks

It is indeed encouraging that on a nationwide scale, new or trimmed content of textbooks is being discussed in the endeavour to reduce the NCERT syllabus by half. Parents are anxious and teachers are still thinking of the implications. Children are expecting better days ahead.

Generating high-quality textbooks: The central core of information is vested in textbooks. Then comes the quality of teaching, learning, and assimilation with focused attention. Textbooks are generally perceived as reading materials that must be mastered, often to be memorised by rote, to sail through examinations, ensuring the successful 'completion' of study.

Their impact on future generations and the destiny of the nation often escapes the attention of most parents. Planning and writing a textbook is a professional process requiring high levels of sensitivity, comprehension and empathy, apart from the competence and commitment. The writers, publishers, and educationists recommending textbooks and their publishing are part of the process of influencing the level of education and future of the country. Not everyone recognises this responsibility.

A small but significant personal experience illustrates a couple of these aspects—an NCERT textbook for class 3 students had a quarter-page sketch titled, *The farmer is ploughing the field*. As director of the NCERT, I received this letter: 'I am a student of class 5. I was teaching my brother, who is in class 3. In this book, the caption under the sketch on page… is incorrect. You must correct your mistake!'

In the sketch, the farmer was seen with the plough on his shoulder, and a pair of bullocks standing nearby! Within half an hour, my handwritten response was mailed to the bright alert 'older brother', acknowledging the error, apologising, and congratulating him for the initiative, besides also requesting him to convey my regards and respects to his teachers, and parents. Manuscripts pass through several stages of scrutiny, and even then, such an error slipped through unseen and unchecked! The entire text was reviewed and re-checked. To ensure effective learning outcomes, every textbook requires sharp scrutiny, assessment, and revision.

NCERT's role and contribution: The NCERT has been enriched with more than sixty years of experience in practically every aspect of school and teacher education, which could indeed be unparalleled amongst institutions and organisations with similar responsibilities anywhere. It can claim the credit for ushering in the process of educational reforms at the national and state level. It has not only dexterously prepared curricula and syllabi, but has also trained experts in textbook writing, evaluation of learning achievements, CCE and annual evaluation, gender sensitivity, and others.

In public perception, it is often remembered, praised, and even criticised mostly for its textbooks. The discussion in 2018 around the HRD Minister's statement on reducing curriculum load has also been shifted to curtailing the size and volume of NCERT textbooks. The NCERT is an advisory body, not a statutory one. Every school education board has the authority to take its own decision in matters of curriculum, syllabus, examinations, and other related issues.

The basic premise is that the NCERT shall set up levels and standards. Every state board must then aim at ensuring compatibility with these so that children are not put to any disadvantage at national level competitions. This has been achieved more or less, because of the close links established over the decades between the NCERT, state level agencies, and experts from various parts of the country.

The process of load reduction shall involve practically every agency working in the areas of education policies, programmes, teaching and evaluation, material development, IT induction, pedagogical implications and several other aspects. The major objective in reducing the avoidable curriculum is to encourage curiosity, creativity, innovations and entrepreneurship. Great attention shall have to be paid to transform the content, pedagogy and work culture of each and every teacher education institution. And that, indeed, is a real tough task.

While textbooks have to be redone and may become leaner, practical experiences must be greatly enhanced and innovations encouraged. The face of teacher preparation institutions must undergo transformation. Should every teacher trainee not be spending at least one hour on the play field every day if he has to ensure the participation of school children willingly in sports and games? One could safely state that ninety percent of these institutions pay little attention to physical fitness and participation in on-the-field activities! You can expect no visible change in the learning environment in schools if teacher-education institutions permit purchase of lesson plans and project work from the market, just to complete the formalities!

Textbooks are no longer the only resource available to students and teachers. The role and the presence of teachers shall become more significant and valuable as children realise that they require guidance and counselling in charting out the correct course and sifting relevant information from the loads of information and knowledge that is now available out of machines. Every teacher shall require more intensive application of his professional competence and skills that shall have to be renewed, upgraded and refurbished continuously. New textbooks, apart from focusing only on reducing load, could also remember certain other responsibilities that are emerging in the fast-changing scenario in education.

To err is human and textbook writers are no exception. The day a textbook is out of the press, it is ready for revision. It may include corrections, additions of new and necessary inputs and, simultaneously, removal of redundant and obsolete content. It is a continuous process and this is the strong point of any organisation or publishing house dealing with textbooks. Dynamic and hence distinguished systems of education are ever ready to take the next step ahead. And that guarantees success.

The Issue of Medium of Instruction

India is known for its economic, social, cultural, ethnic, linguistic, and religious diversities and it should commit to transform its education system to achieve social cohesion and religious harmony, and thereby strengthen unity in diversity. Its education system has to encompass a very sensitive canvas. Its three-language formula, which was accepted in the mid-1960s, is yet to be implemented fully in letter and spirit.

India's national policy of education was last revisited in 1992. After more than a quarter of a century, in 2019, the Kasturirangan Committee presented its draft report to the GOI for finalisation of the new National Education Policy. Preparation of this report was preceded by a national consultation process spread over four years.

Everyone is concerned about education, its quality, utility, and capacity to achieve total personality development. There is no limit to improvement in the presentation of such reports, but implementation has to begin at some point. The NEP-2020 consists mostly of formulations that deserve the support of all, and active involvement of academics and scholars, who are unconstrained by ideological bonds and narrow political considerations. The report attempts comprehensive articulation of national expectations and aspirations fully harmonised and synchronised with international trends and requirements. The vision of India's new education system has accordingly been crafted to ensure that it touches the life of each and every citizen, and is consistent with their ability to contribute to many growing developmental imperatives of this country on the one hand, and towards creating a just and equitable society on the other. To achieve such an objective, the language and medium of instruction are very relevant.

It was interesting that within hours of the presentation of the report to the HRD minister, and its simultaneous uploading on the Ministry's website, certain vested interests attempted to create an unsavoury conflict in the minds of people, raising the issue of the so-called imposition of Hindi in non-Hindi-speaking states. It goes to the credit of the MHRD that it issued a clarification that the government has no intention to impose any language on any set of people unwilling to learn it. In fact, ever since the three-language formula was accepted by the GOI and a commitment made to the nation, the Union government has never tried to impose any language hegemony.

The issue of the medium of education being the mother tongue has been comprehensively addressed in the NEP-2020. It is accepted that the initial education must be provided in the mother tongue of the child. It is also acknowledged that children have an extremely good capacity to learn multiple languages in the early-age group of 2 to 8 years. The NEP Report states:

> Language has a direct bearing as the mediator in all cognitive and social capacities, including in knowledge acquisition and production. The science of child development and language acquisition suggests that young children become literate in (as a language) and learn best through (as medium of instruction) their 'local language', that is, the language spoken at home.

It is interesting that the Committee uses two terms, mother tongue and the language spoken at home. An illustrative example indicates the level of fascination for English medium schools in India, particularly among those who can afford to pay the exorbitant fees in these privately managed public schools!

A young professor, working in a national academic institution in Delhi, sought a transfer to his hometown in Bangalore, to look after his octogenarian in-laws who had no other support. The request was accepted, and the family shifted to their home town. Their two children, ten and twelve years old, easily got admission in a public school. The grandparents could only communicate in Kannada, while the children could only speak English. The young parents' response was very truthful, and revealing as they said that 'We decided to speak only English in our home and family conversation, even with guests to ensure that the children acquire greater fluency in English. This was all for their bright future, and to make it easier for them to go overseas.'

This focus on speaking English has inspired the mushrooming growth of several English-medium schools in large villages and towns across the country.

Practically every commission and committee appointed in the post-Independence period, did accept and emphasise the importance and necessity of the mother tongue. However, the failure to maintain mother tongue medium in government schools is now being addressed under the school merger plan. The system understands the ground reality. It will be interesting to see what finally emerges on the language front and the issue of the medium of instruction in the final national policy.

Basic Education and the New Education Policy

India is in the implementation phase of NPE-2020, that envisions an education system rooted in the Indian ethos that contributes directly to transforming India, that is Bharat, sustainably into an equitable and vibrant knowledge society, by providing high-quality education to all, and thereby making India a global superpower. It is a tall order, but a critical necessity to let the benefits of education reach the 'last man in the line', who has been waiting for generations to get basic human amenities, human dignity, and an opportunity to make his or contribution to national growth and development. Finalised after over four years and an extensive and intensive nation-wide consultation process, the policy expects the curricula and pedagogy to be radically transformed to instil a deep sense of respect towards the fundamental duties and constitutional values that every citizen must discharge towards the country, besides bonding with one's country and infusing a sense of conscious awareness of one's roles and responsibilities in a changing world. The bonding with the country, and an inherent sense of pride in its people is doubly emphasised, not limiting it only to thought, but extending it to the Spirit, intellect and deeds. as the aim is also to develop knowledge, skills, values, and dispositions that support responsible commitment to human rights, sustainable development and living, and global well-being, thereby reflecting a truly global feeling in every citizen. This beautiful tree must be nourished to bloom fully. Towards that end, the new education policy must be scrutinised to ascertain whether it would link Indians to India and to what extent it would give young Indians not only degrees and certificates but also the knowledge, skills and a personality to move ahead in life with self-assurance, dignity, and spirit of adventure.

Teachers and the National Education Policy

The process of the Kasturirangan Committee on the NEP was initiated in 2015. The NEP was formally approved by the cabinet on 29 July 2020. In a welcome move, the draft that was both in English and Hindi—was promptly put up on the ministry's website. It is an outcome of nationwide consultations that extended over three and a half years. It must be appreciated across the board that the MHRD again invited inputs that people, institutions, organisations, experts and others may like to submit after going through the Policy. The report clearly indicates how critically relevant it has become in the globalised world we live in, to ensure active dynamism in the formulation of the education policy to ensure it remains relevant to absorb the challenges that are emerging before nations at an unprecedented pace.

The deliberations, before and after the finalisation of the policy—shall invariably make references to the earlier education policies, particularly those of 1968, 1986 and 1992. The contents of these earlier reports, at least in academic and professional circles, shall be scrutinised in the context of what was proposed, and to what extent it was really achieved in actual implementation. Chapter five of the NEP-2020 on 'Teachers' begins with the objective outlined in the policy, chiefly to:

> Ensure that all students at all levels of school education are taught by passionate, motivated, highly qualified, professionally trained, and well-equipped teachers.

This is a very well thought-out comprehensive policy statement that encompasses every aspect of what a child, community or society expects from a teacher.

Things have changed in the modern world and India and Indians are merged into this modernisation. The knowledge quest is now often pursued with the sole and primary commercial considerations, whether it is getting a patent first, or taking over the market! Historical interventions impeded Indian knowledge traditions, and today, we are just copying the trends of much-glamourised globalisation.

There is another side of the coin. From those 30 per cent students that qualify from Indian schools, often their academic acumen is considered good enough for them to get admission, even scholarships, in well-known HEIs overseas. The quest, in fact, is to keep them back here to study further in HEIs in India. Many students from other countries seek admission in India's HEIs. Young Indians have excelled practically in every field including ICT, space sciences, and in several potential areas that could change the world for the better. The horizon of good quality education is presently available, however, roughly to only one-third of students; it needs to be extended to all, and extended fast.

Educationally alert countries are conscious of the pace of change all around, and the need to prepare their young generation for a highly competitive world. While we need to combat prevailing malpractices in the education system, we need to also look around and observe how conditions are being improved globally. Like other educationally advanced nations, we must put into practice the adage that the investment in education pays the highest returns. No nation could remain slow and reticent on this count. Even if India is late on certain counts of efficacy and improvement, she must invigorate the system with new ideas and initiatives, even in tough conditions.

Chapter 6

Inculcating Research Culture in the Learning Process

Universities are primarily the centres of knowledge acquisition, creation, establishing its utility, and its transfer to future generations. In the Indian tradition of the knowledge quest, one must immediately add that knowledge and skills so acquired must be used for the welfare of humanity: *Sarva bhut hite ratah*! This ought to be the universal goal but is not so in actual practice. At this juncture of human history, materialistic pursuits have overtaken spiritual quests; 'learning to earn' is the keyword for both individuals and institutions.

This in direct contrast to the universal perception that education and its institutions must develop good, thoughtful, well-rounded and creative individuals of developed character. At the societal level, it must contribute to creating a socially conscious, knowledgeable, and skilled nation. The NEP-2020 intends to transform its HES in approach, structure, processes and learner outcomes, i.e., products. It has been specifically stated in the NEP-2020 (p. 45):

> Knowledge creation and research are critical in growing and sustaining a large and vibrant economy, uplifting

society, and continuously inspiring a nation to achieve even greater heights. Indeed, some of the most prosperous civilisations (such as India, Mesopotamia, Egypt and Greece) to the modern era (such as the United States, Germany, Israel, South Korea, and Japan) were are strong knowledge societies that attained intellectual and material wealth in large part through celebrated and fundamental contributions to new knowledge in the realm of science as well as arts, language, and culture that enhanced and uplifted not only their own civilisations but others around the globe.

Never before, was a robust eco-system of research more important to India than at present. So much is changing at an unprecedented pace; so many issues and concerns are threatening the very survival of the human race on Planet Earth that only a sustained and well-directed comprehensive effort to move towards a knowledge society could ensure, 'economic, intellectual, societal, environmental, and technological health and progress of a nation.' Creation of a research culture that could respond to all the expectations of the people has to be examined in light of the most critical input, namely, investment in education. The NEP-2020 highlights this through the following para:

> Despite this critical importance of research, the research and innovation investment in India is, at the current time, only 0.69 per cent of GDP as compared to 2.8 per cent in the United States of America, 4.3 per cent in Israel and 4.2 per cent in South Korea.

One genuinely expects it to be enhanced and augmented from sources other than the governments.

Motivation

It is universally acknowledged that best research output emerges from a multidisciplinary university setting. It happens when a strong culture of research and knowledge creation is built up. It invariably leads to best teaching and learning processes not only in higher education, but impacts school education also. It is indeed encouraging to note that India has realised the need of creating an organic relationship between research and school education. The NEP-2020 envisages, 'Definitive shifts in school education to a more play and discovery based-style of learning with emphasis on the scientific method and critical thinking.' Qualitative transformation in higher education and research just cannot be achieved without a sound base of good quality school education.

These ideas and their articulation in the current context could be better comprehended in the light of some of the learned discourses by luminaries who dazzled the sphere of research through their own dedication and commitment and gave precious gifts of knowledge that paved the path for a better human future. These continue to inspire generations to explore, extract and achieve more and more from hitherto unfathomed treasures from the oceans of knowledge. Delivering an address at the sixtieth birthday celebrations of eminent scientist, Max Planck in 1918, Einstein referred to classes of people who take science, study and research; for some it was a sense of joyful superior intellectual power, and those, 'Who have offered the products of their brains on this altar for purely utilitarian purposes.'

He elaborated that in the 'Temple of Science', with its many mansions, if these were the only two categories, only creepers would grow! Why are others in the sciences, the one discipline that brings fragrance of sublime life to humanity? Einstein quotes Schopenhauer in 1954, implying that one of the strongest motives that lead men to art and science is escape from everyday life with its painful, crudity and hopeless dreariness, from the fetters of 'one's own ever shifting desires'. Here is what he said:

> Townsman's irresistible longing to escape from his noisy, cramped surroundings into silence of high mountains, where the eyes range freely through the still, pure air and fondly traces out the restful contours apparently built for eternity.

Then he goes on to mention the real positive motive:

> Man tries to make for himself in the fashion that suits him best a simplified and intelligible picture of the world; he then tries to some extent to substitute this cosmos of his for the world of experience, and thus to overcome it. This is what the painter, the poet, the speculative philosopher, and the natural scientist do, each in his own fashion.

This was said several decades ago, but if a survey is conducted on, 'how, why, who, and what for' of research in science and other sectors—in an age of multidisciplinarity—the outcomes could be classified more precisely, but the essence would not change. Human urge for security, emotional support, and peace is the core motivation for higher order intellectual, innovative and entrepreneurial initiatives. If one moves ahead in time, and comes to 1979, the articulation appears more familiar. In a 1991 lecture titled, 'Beauty and the Quest for Beauty in Science', S Chandrasekhar referred to the illustrious scientist Poincare:

> The scientist does not study nature because it is useful to

do so. He studies it because he takes pleasure in it; and he takes pleasure in it because it is beautiful. If nature were not beautiful, it would not be worth knowing and life would not be worth living.... I mean the intimate beauty which comes from the harmonious order of its parts and which a pure intelligence can grasp.

Man has explored the vastness of stars, galaxies, space, and the cosmos beginning with a telescope, on the one hand, and also with the vastness of the smallest device, a microscope! Humans have explored–and this is an eternal process–to look within and beyond.

Research is a Cautious Quest

At present, research is supposed to begin only after attaining a post-graduate qualification. In the proposed setup and introduction of four-year undergraduate courses, it could be initiated in the fourth year, and after completing it, could be continued for a doctoral degree. It helps in settling down in a job, for one, and those who continue later, are serious scholars, learned academics and intellectuals. A truly inspired person could be doing research without any formal qualifications, pursuing his idea of exploration, gaining more comprehension of things around him, or those inspired by his imagination. It is imagination, ideas, curiosity and creativity that gel together and lead to an output that may surprise the creator himself. Those in the formal informed systems, familiar with the latest developments in the area need to realise the power of the human imagination, so lucidly articulated by Einstein:

> Imagination is more important than knowledge. For knowledge is limited, whereas imagination embraces

the entire world, stimulating progress, giving birth to evolution. (Swami Tathagatananda, 2013: 21)

We are all familiar with great advances in sciences and their applications that have transformed human lives all around. However, these alone cannot enhance the Human Happiness Index, as 'Humanity has every reason to place the proclaimers of high moral standards and values above the discoveries of objective truth.'

On several occasions, Einstein expressed his ideas and concerns about morality and ethics with an intensity that flows direct from the heart:

> The most important human endeavour is the striving for morality in our actions. Our inner balance and even our existence depend on it. Only morality in our actions can give beauty and dignity to life. To make this a living force and bring it to clear consciousness is perhaps the foremost task of education. The foundation of morality should not be made dependent on myth tied to any authority lest any doubt about the myth or legitimacy of the authority imperil the foundation of sound judgement and action. (ibid.:174).

He, like so many others, could see the symphony of scientific growth and developments, and the independence of thought from prejudices and authoritarian interference. Scientific developments and their technological imperatives have changed the contours of human life. But hunger, poverty and ill-health continue to disrupt the lives of billions even today. Further, these advances have not led to the universalisation of the dignity of life to every human being. The Eastern philosophy of *Aparigraha:* non-accumulation, increasingly offers a ray of hope to entire humanity in these times of unprecedented pace of change ushered in by the developments in ICT. Could it be because of the 'modern people who neglect or disobey the laws of spiritual development?'

From Einstein, let us now go back to Swami Vivekananda who opined:

> It is one of the evils of civilisation that we are after intellectual education alone and take no care of the heart. It only makes man ten times more selfish, and that will be our destruction.... Intellect can never become inspired: only the heart when it is enlightened becomes inspired. An intellectual heartless man never becomes an inspired man.... Intellect has been cultured, with the result that hundreds of sciences have been discovered, and their effect has been that few have made slaves of many that is all the good that has been done. (ibid.:16).

Everyone is experiencing it and witnessing the manner in which multinationals have captured markets, uprooted millions, calling them 'business partners', when in reality, they have deprived them all of the dignity that was their lone solace as independent workers. So-called research is being sponsored by multinationals, including pharmaceutical companies. Who is not familiar with the objectives behind these endeavours?

Evaluating Research

Let one traverse in the vast and extended knowledge quest that flourished in ancient India and still survives in its continuity and relevance. Recall the Taxila-Nalanda times. There is an anecdote concerning Acharya Bhadant and his disciple (*shishya*) Jivak that gives some idea of the Indian tradition of research and search for knowledge. When the *shishya* evaluated his own learner attainments, he approached the Guru, and informed him that he had completed his studies, and would like to offer *Guru Dakshina* (the traditional custom of 'thanksgiving', a payback to the teacher) that the learned Acharya may prescribe, and then bless him to go back and utilise the knowledge acquired under his feet to serve humanity.

In the form of *Guru Dakshina*, the Guru wanted him to find some herb, shrub, plant, tree, leaf, or any such thing that is of no use in human welfare! This was the 'project work' described in contemporary language and obviously Jivak must have followed a systematic process of project formulation, decided upon the delimitations, formulated hypotheses, done experimentation, observation, tabulation, and so on. No details are, however, available of how he went about executing his project. However, he reported back, after a reasonable gap, that he could not find anything that grows on earth that cannot be used for human welfare! What a finding! What an articulation of man-nature mutuality. And what a way of inspiration to create new knowledge! The guru knew it, but made the *shishya* 'discover' it for himself.

That is what Swami Vivekananda has explained that no one can actually 'teach' anyone, for the learner it is all discovery from within, the manifestation of the perfection already in man. There is enough evidence, despite the glossing over for several centuries, of India's contribution in varied fields of science, mathematics, astronomy, social sciences, and the spiritual domains. All this would have never been possible if India had not learnt to seek beauty in its totality: *Satyam, Shivam, Sundaram*; Truth, Goodness, Beauty. One may like to see its reflections in the heart-warming lines of

poet Keats (as referred to by Chandrashekhar, 1991: 65).
Beauty is truth, truth beauty – that is all Ye know on Earth and shall ye need to know.

And beauty manifests itself only in quiet, compassion, cohesion, correlation, and composure, and needs goodness and peace around it. Are the researchers experiencing this?

Inculcating a culture of research requires a continuity right from the initial years. The NEP-2020 has recommended nurturing of the talent and traits by creating continuity right from 3+ years onwards. Here one needs to remember three of the basics taught to us by Sri Aurobindo:
1. From near to far.
2. Nothing can be taught.
3. Mind must be consulted in its own development.

If teachers can comprehend their role in this light, they become partners in learning and in discovering. As Swami Vivekananda said, whatever a child learns is, in fact, a discovery from within! To this, add the touching prescription of Gurudev Rabindranath Tagore that every child is blessed with two boons by God and nature: the power of ideas and the power of imagination. Sadly enough, our education systems invariably make every conscious effort to impede these!

This is best exemplified by the board examinations or by the evaluation and assessment system, practically in every context. We have not even developed a transparent teacher-recruitment systems as yet. This poses a great challenge to researchers. The concern is best exemplified by an instance from outside India that indicates how teacher-educators and teachers must be sensitive to the finer intricacies and to the subsequent consequences of an infirm evaluation. Richard

Feynman, returning after receiving his Nobel Prize, decided to visit his school, as a gesture of gratitude. Excited school authorities dug out his performance records and found that his IQ was 'fairly low' at that time! Reaching home, Feynman told his wife that, 'To win Nobel Prize was of little significance, but the fact that he had won it despite such a low IQ was something great.'

Any teacher with experience can recall similar instances from among the various students he or she has taught over the years and can give examples of students of who succeeded beyond expectations. Mohandas Karamchand Gandhi's IQ may never have been measured in his school, but he was certainly not considered a brilliant learner, and was obstinate enough not to copy the spelling of 'kettle', because he did not know it, despite clear hints from his teacher. The instances of Steve Job and Bill Gates are well-known to every aspiring young graduate, all over the world. Even Albert Einstein belonged to the category of those whose real potential was unrecognised in their formal learning days.

Researchers are, generally speaking, considered intellectuals of the highest calibre who deserve respect bordering on adulation. They have to remain committed and conscious of the credibility of their profession. What Albert Einstein said to intellectuals would be very relevant to young persons engaged in research in the fast-changing scenario in every sector of human activity and endeavour:

> By painful experience we have learnt that rational thinking does not suffice to solve the problem of our social life. Penetrating research and keen scientific work have often had tragic implications for mankind, producing, on the one hand, inventions which liberated man from exhausting physical labour, making his life easier and richer; but on

the other hand, introducing a graver restlessness into his life, making him a slave to technological environment, and—most catastrophic of all—creating the means for his own mass destruction. This indeed is a tragedy of overwhelming poignancy. (op. cit.: 148).

This indicates how research in the sciences leads to social, economic and cultural, and security imperatives. Once again, we are forced to recall the debacle of the atomic bombing of Hiroshima and Nagasaki after the successful atomic explosion at Las Alamos! The way the world was shaping out after WWII disgusted Einstein, as he witnessed the race for producing self-annihilating weapons; the increase in violence not only continued in his lifetime but remains uncontrolled till today. So much of resources and efforts are being invested in this sector!

Finally, research, innovations, entrepreneurship, and acquiring skills in the present is what will lead our future generations towards peace, tranquillity, and human values. The production of new knowledge is an eternal instinctive human pursuit, and it shall continue ever after. In the context of implementing its new education policy, India will be working on the newly suggested transformations in the categorisation of universities, bringing its regulatory bodies under one umbrella: and in the creation of the National Research Foundation (NRF). However, quality enhancement is invariably a consequence of the growth of good quality schools, and value attached to total personality development, character formation, and internalised commitment of children in schools. In the Indian context, over 60 per cent schools are functioning under severe conditions of deprivation and deficiency, with rapidly declining credibility and public acceptance. All nations have learnt by experience that maximum returns accrue only through investment in education, and focus on innovations, entrepreneurship, and research. Imagine the massive enhancements in quality research output in India if all schools were functioning at professionally and academically acceptable, if not optimum levels? We also need universities that are autonomous with academics and researchers conscious of their roles as *Acharyas*, who would ideally be emulated by the young. The Indian education system must strive hard to achieve these goals at the earliest.

Chapter 7

Covid-19 and Its Impact

Almost as soon as the NEP-2020 was presented as the future of education in India, the global Covid pandemic took over. From the beginning of 2020, right through 2021, and in 2022, the Covid-19 pandemic raged, introducing unprecedented and unforeseen changes in the systems of education, globally. The tradition of 'going-to-school' saw the paradigm shift as the 'going' now meant facing the screen of a laptop, a tablet, or phone as online classes became the norm. 'Locked down' and home-bound students have had to struggle in far too many ways, and have had to deal with a diverse range of uncertainties and concerns.

In an article, released on 13 May 2020, Stefania Giannini, the UNESCO assistant director-general for Education, and others, explained the magnitude of the problem. Corona school closures impacted more than 1.5 billion children and 90 per cent of the world's student population:

> 'Closures happened in quick succession as a measure to contain the Covid-19 virus. Just as speedily, governments deployed measures for learning to continue through

platforms, television and radio in what has been the most far-reaching experiment in the history of education. But when it comes to reopening of schools, the tempo is far more uncertain. According to UNESCO data, 100 countries have not yet announced a date for schools to reopen, 65 have plans for partial or full reopening, while 32 will end the academic year online. For 890 million students however, the school calendar has never been so undefined. (World bank blog)

One of the most sensitive and serious concerns consequent to the Corona pandemic, and one that was been debated all over, was how and when to re-open schools! Almost all parents, continued to wait and watch, all through most of 2021, while different countries offered different rationales for delaying openings of schools.

In India, the scenario was definitely one of hesitation and concern. As many as 250 million children study in Indian schools. Several parents were clear: even if an academic year was lost, that was preferred to the risk of contracting the disease. The level of anxiety and uncertainty was very clearly evident in a 2020 study in 224 districts on a sample of 18,000 parents. Thirty-seven per cent very clearly indicated that they would send their wards to school only when there are no cases for 21 days continuously within the district and within a 20-km radius of the school! Another 20 per cent would send their children to school when there was no case in the country for 21 days, 16 per cent would do so only 21 days after no case was reported in the state; 13 per cent would wait till a vaccine was developed!

The HRD Ministry acknowledged that the decision of reopening schools was the prerogative of the state governments, as they would take the call based on the situation in their states. The Union Ministry issued guidelines on sanitation, quarantine, physical distancing and other relevant details. Uncertainty loomed large on the education system. Creative minds worked on possible solutions that could help combat disruptions in this unprecedented teaching-learning scenario.

As a precautionary measure in the wake of the Covid-19 pandemic, the MHRD on 18 March 2020, issued directions to UGC, AICTE, NTA, NIOS, CBSE, NCTE and all autonomous organisations under it for the postponement of all examinations till 31 March 2020. (PIB) The biggest testing ground was when the Board examinations for classes 10 and 12 were scheduled to take place. In compliance of the instructions received from MHRD, Government of India, dated 18 March 2020, CBSE postponed all the board examinations that were to be held between 19 and 31 March 2020. CBSE was further advised to promote all students studying in classes 1 to 8 to the next class/grade. Students of classes 9 and 11 were to be promoted to the next class/grade based on their school-based assessments including projects, periodic tests, and term exams, conducted thus far. The Ministry also recommended conducting board examinations only for 29 main subjects required for promotion and maybe crucial for admissions in HEIs. Instructions for marking and for assessments in all such cases were issued separately by the Board.

The Ministry issued regular guidelines and Standard Operating Procedures (SOPs) for enabling education to all students during Covid restrictions, such as the Pragyata Guidelines (for digital education) and the academic calendar. The Ministry of Home Affairs (MHA), in an official order dated 30 September 2020, stated that State/UT Governments may take a decision in respect of re-opening of schools, after 15 October 2020, in a graded manner. The decision would have to be taken in consultation with the respective school and institution's management, based on their assessment of the situation.

As the uncertain conditions due to Covid continued in 2021, the Prime Minister chaired a review meeting regarding Class 12 Board exams of CBSE on 1 June 2021. Based on extensive consultation and feedback received from all stakeholders, including State governments, it was decided that the Class 12 Board Exams would not be held during 2021. The PM reasserted that students, parents, and teachers were naturally worried about the health of the students in the prevailing situation of the pandemic. Students could not be forced to appear for exams in such a stressful situation. It was also decided that CBSE would take steps to compile the results of class 12 students as per a well-defined objective criteria in a time-bound manner.

After the Class 12 Board Exams were cancelled, CBSE developed a policy for the tabulation of marks with the help of an expert committee. This was then approved by the Hon'ble Supreme Court of India in a writ petition, Civil No. 522, dated 17 June 2021. The MoE regularly monitored the vaccination of the teaching and non-teaching staff to ensure confidence and thus creating an enabling environment for schools to move towards reopening. In November 2021, a majority of the states opened the schools for all classes. Over 92 per cent of teaching staff had been vaccinated by then. In the institutions under the Central Government, over 96 per cent of the teaching staff were vaccinated (PIB).

The Ministry of Home Affairs Order dated 30 September

2020 directed that all states could begin to reopen schools from 15 October 2020, in a phased approach, except in identified containment zones. The UGC guidelines on examinations and the academic calendar, in view of the Covid-19 pandemic were initially issued on 29 April 2020, advising universities to plan their academic activities keeping in view the safety and interest of all stakeholders, giving highest priority to the health of all concerned, while adopting and implementing the guidelines. Universities were requested to establish a cell for handling grievances of students related to examinations and other academic activities that had arisen due to the pandemic and to coordinate with the students.

To further monitor queries, grievances, and other academic matters of students, teachers, and institutions, UGC had also set up a dedicated helpline number. Students could also lodge grievances on the Online Students Grievance Redressal Portal (https://www.ugc.ac.in/ grievance/student_reg.aspx).

The UGC issued revised guidelines for examination and an academic calendar on 6 July 2020, wherein universities were required to chart out a plan for completion of terminal semester/final year examinations by the end of September 2020 in offline (pen & paper)/ online/blended (online+offline) mode following the prescribed protocols/guidelines related to the pandemic. In September 2020, guidelines on the academic calendar for first year UG and PG students in the universities and colleges were issued. Yet another set of revised guidelines were issued on 16 July 2021.

The All India Council for Teacher Education (AICTE) offered 49 free online courses such as GATE Exam Preparation, Free App-based courses for communication skills and interview preparation, Certified Full Stack

Engineer, Digital Marketing, Java Programming, Diploma in Machine Learning with R studio, Online Internship in Financial Analysis Basics, On-line Engineering Teaching Resources, etc. There are over 100 hours of video lessons on all the major topics of each branch of engineering (*Hindustan Times*, 2020).

As per a UNESCO-UNICEF, *India Case Study: Situation Analysis on the Effects of and Responses to Covid-19 on the Education Sector in Asia:*

> The Government has made huge efforts to respond to the effects of Covid-19, and its commitment to education is reflected in the 2020 NEP, published despite the pandemic. Its decentralised approach to dealing with the effects of Covid-19 makes sense in such a populous and diverse country, and some states have developed approaches that could be usefully replicated elsewhere. The importance of using digital technology in future is stressed in both the NEP and in the response to Covid-19, but there are many reasons why digitalisation will only provide part of the educational infrastructure in future. Addressing the learning loss suffered by children during school closures, particularly children from poor and displaced families, will be critical to recovery.

Chapter 8

Digital Transformation of Education Systems

The 'regular' and accepted scenarios of education, work, and communication were all drastically challenged with the global experience of the pandemic. For the first time, work-from-home (WFH) became a totally accepted norm, to the extent that even in the present day, when the 'restrictions' imposed due to the strict precautions related with Covid-19 have been relaxed, several organisations are continuing with the WFH protocol as it is now happily accepted. The pros of avoiding long commutes to the work-place, the time saved, and the convenient feasability of meetings on *Zoom*, *Google Meet*, *Skype*, *FaceTime*, and other digitally viable platforms have ensured that WFH will continue to be a very viable option, at least for private enterprise.

But when it comes to schools and HEIs, the environment of children and youth interacting, one-on-one with teachers and each other, in classrooms and on the playground, makes the entire experience of proactive learning irreplaceable. The education system is very closely geared to physical communcation and interaction, and the 'on-line' process was always seen as the best alternative in a bad situation. But nonetheless it took on a key role for some time, and peaked during 2020-2022.

On-line Studies

The manner digital learning was initiated by a large number of schools, with online classes, and webinars, during the 'lock-down' stretch triggered by the pandemic, and how quickly teachers adapted, indicated the swiftness with which the system realised the complex nature of the concerns and explored all the alternatives. It, however, was not an easy task.

On the one hand, we have schools in India that are well-equipped on all counts, comparable to the best anywhere. But on the other end of the spectrum, we also have schools that are perpetually deficient, even deprived, both on the infrastructure side as also in professional support. Over the last three decades, the alarming shortage of teachers in schools, which directly impacts the quality of learning has been a cause of considerable concern. This adversely impacts the credibility of schools besides the very obvious inadequate teaching process. The immediate demand on the education system was to focus on evolving new pedagogy and teacher-training strategies.

Many traditional teachers had never gone beyond the blackboard-teaching system, especially so in several middle-level schools. The pandemic instigated reverse migration of workers, who left the metros where they worked to return to their home states and villages. They lost their livelihood and it predominantly impacted the education of their children. Parents of children presently enrolled in high-end English-medium private schools began approaching government schools. The serious churning in the economic structure adversely affected the lower and lower-middle rungs of society.

Such families found themselves at the crossroads, unable to some extent, to manage their economic situation. Many parents were no longer in a position to pay school fees. Meanwhile, the local village school infrastructure, to whatever minimum level it existed, had children seeking to join, despite the fact that they were studying in comparably more structured government schools in the cities. The tussle has continued since then. Again, in the post-pandemic phase, the families who returned to the cities had to struggle to seek fresh admissions. Many had left their families back in the villages as relocating, and getting re-admission proved futile. And yet, private schools remain worried about sustaining their incomes so as to continue with the infrastructure that they are committed to provide.

Several children in remote areas had no access to online classes, or their parents could not afford to buy computers or smart phones. In many regions where there was no internet or wi-fi, children were forced to drop out of school. This tussle shall continue to take varied dimensions in the forthcoming years. While private schools are more worried about sustaining their incomes so that they can continue with the infrastructure they have committed to provide, several rural schools needed to be up and running with new norms and teaching pedagogies.

On the brighter and positive side, there were also several stories of innovative practices adopted by teachers during the lockdown. A teacher in Ghaziabad, Shyna Kara, created her own multimedia content and shared it with students beforehand. This, she said, converted the role of students from 'passive receptors' to 'active participants'. Ten months down the line, she was planning to continue using her 'flipped classroom' technique as the schools were reopening (*Indian Express*, 6 February 2021).

The Digital Wave

The pedagogy underwent unprecedented changes, and teachers already serving in schools geared up to learn new skills. While tools and techniques changed, sometimes beyond recognition, the pedagogical principles however, remained the same.

Therefore, to ensure uninterrupted teaching-learning during the lockdown period, requisite measures were taken by autonomous institutions to safeguard the academic interest of students. Several digital initiatives were started urgently with the objective of ensuring uninterrupted learning. Among the endeavours initiated were:

- PM e-Vidya that unifies all efforts related to digital/online/on-air education
- Diksha, Digital Infrastructure for Knowledge Sharing, an initiative of the National Council of Educational Research and Training (NCERT, Ministry of Education);
- Swayam Prabha, a group of 34 DTH channels devoted to telecasting high-quality educational programmes on a 24x7 basis using the GSAT-15 satellite
- IIT PAL, video lectures for classes 11 and 12, prepared by IIT professors and subject experts to help students to better understand the subjects in their self-study endeavours, so as to do well in competitive examinations
- The Kendriya Vidyalaya Sangathan (KVS) adopted online and digital methods for teaching and directed its regional offices to find ways for engaging students in online learning (PIB, 2020). KVS teachers conducted

online classes for live sessions on three DTH channels- Panini, Sharda and Kishore Manch, all part of the Swayam Prabha endeavour, with a group of 32 DTH channels as already mentioned above
- Skype and live web chats were also used to address student's queries and clear their doubts
- The National Institute of Open Schooling (NIOS) and NCERT started providing online lessons through the (Study Webs of Active-Learning for Young Aspiring Minds-Massive Open Online Courses) SWAYAM-MOOC platform in all major subjects at the secondary and senior secondary level
- Tata Sky and Airtel DTH operators came forward to air three Swayam Prabha DTH channels on their DTH platforms
- Besides, DD-DTH and Jio TV App, Panini, Sharda and Kishore Manch Swayam Prabha DTH channels were soon available through all DTH service providers
- Study material for the differently-abled was developed by NIOS on Digitally Accessible Information System (DAISY) and in sign language

The ICT initiatives of the Ministry of Education (MoE) Erstwhile Ministry of Human Resource Development (MHRD), UGC and its Inter University Centres (IUCs), Information and Library Network (INFLIBNET) and the Consortium for Educational Communication (CEC), in the form of digital platforms were shared and teachers, students and researchers in universities and colleges could access these for broadening their horizons of learning and knowledge sharing. Through all the communications by the MoE and UGC, it was emphasised that teaching-learning processes using online modes should continue through Google Classroom, Cisco Webex Meeting, YouTube streaming, OERs, SWAYAM platform (www.swayam.gov.in), Swayam Prabha (www.swayamprabha.gov.in) (available on Doordarshan [Free dish] and Dish TV), e-yantra (www.e-yantra.org), Virtual Labs (www.vlab.co.in), FOSSEE (https://fossee.in), application of spoken tutorials (www.spoken-tutorial.org), National Digital Library (NDL) (https://ndl.iitkgp. ac.in), and electronic journals (https://ess.inflibnet.ac.in).

In July 2020, the MoE released the India Report on Digital Education (*PIB*, 2020) which covered the innovative methods adopted by the MoE and the Education Departments of States and Union Territories for ensuring accessible and inclusive education to children at home and reducing learning gaps. Several media tools were used to connect with learners, some major ones being social media favourites like WhatsApp groups for learners of all classes, online classes through the *YouTube* channel, *Google Meet*, *Skype*, *E-learning portals*, TV (Doordarshan and regional channels), and Radio (*AIR*). To facilitate remote learning, several innovative mobile apps and portals were also launched by some states. As per the report, using WhatsApp as a medium for education and to encourage teachers, parents, and students to stay connected proved to be an innovative initiative of the states (PIB, 2020).

In order to reach out to students with low bandwidth or with no internet, or with limited access to digital means, the report mentions the extensive use of the *Swayam Prabha DTH channels* and radio including community radio for ensuring round-the-clock education to students. Broadcasting radio talks for students of primary classes in their mother tongue is a very essential add-on.

Enumerating some of the steps taken by the Government to make online education more conducive, the Minister of State for Education, informed the Rajya Sabha in July 2022, of the Samagra Shiksha Scheme of the Department of School Education and Literacy, which aims to ensure inclusive and equitable quality education at all levels of school education, extending from pre-school to class 12. Implemented in partnership with all the states and UTs, the scheme provides financial assistance to them for various components including the strengthening of ICT infrastructure in schools. Under Samagra Shiksha, the ICT component envisages covering all government and government-aided schools from classes 6 to 12 and Teacher Education Institutions (TEIs) as well, subject to adequate budgetary provision.

The options for schools: These include ICT or smart classrooms for schools, which have not availed the ICT facility earlier, according to their requirement and need. An additional ICT lab can also be considered for schools with more than 700 students on their rolls.

Another option is that schools which have already availed the ICT facility earlier can opt for classrooms/tablets as per the norms of the scheme. Financial support of Rs. 10,000 per teacher for tablets is being provided from the year 2022-23 to the teachers at the primary level, based on state-specific proposals as part of 'Learning Recovery Package'. The ICT component covers government and government-aided schools with classes from 6 to 12, which will enable the use of ICT resources from younger grades. The ICT Labs are approved in 120,614 schools and Smart classrooms are approved in 82,120 schools. A total of 14,82,565 tablets have been sanctioned to the teachers dealing with primary classes.

The MoE issued the Pragyata guidelines to the states and UTs to facilitate continued education through various modes. The guidelines inter-alia include situations where internet connectivity is not available or is available with very less bandwidth, and where resources are shared through various platforms like television, radio etc. that do not depend on the internet. Similarly, Students Learning Enhancement Guidelines were released in 2020 to support learning of children during Covid-19. Guidelines for development of e-content for children with special needs have been released. Guidelines for parent participation in home-based learning during school closure and beyond have also been released in 2021.

The MoE also undertook a proactive initiative, named, 'Manodarpan' covering a wide range of activities to provide psychosocial support to students, teachers and families for mental health and emotional wellbeing during the Covid outbreak.

Chapter 9

Towards Transformational Reforms in Education for Vision 2047

India's National Education Policy 2020 (NEP-2020) was launched almost four years ago on 29 July 2020. India celebrated *Azadi ka Amrit Mahotsav* in 2022, commemorating the 75th year of Independence and soon after, suggestions were invited from stakeholders to contribute to preparing an Action Plan and Document of Vision India@2047, as the country gears up to celebrate 100 years of its Independence, in 2047. The aim is to create a roadmap for achieving targets by 2030 with defined outcomes, particularly in the social sector, such as education.

Action Plan and Document on Vision India@2047

The aspirations for India@2047 as outlined in the online survey include:

Attaining new heights of prosperity: This aims at making the best facilities available in villages and cities, eliminating unnecessary government interference in citizens' lives, and building world-class infrastructures.

Action plan and document on Vision India@2047: This focuses on the social sector, including the education sector. Stakeholders such as research institutions, universities, and domain experts have to be involved in brainstorming and preparing the action plan. The plan aims to define targets and outcomes for the decade ending 2030.

Cross-cutting issues: During the deliberation and ideation process, several cross-cutting issues will surely arise. These may include global value chains, leveraging growth in sunrise sectors, climate change, research and development, innovation and entrepreneurship, employment, human capital development, and governance.

Higher education: The institutions and higher education entities under the Department of Higher Education are key stakeholders in achieving new heights of prosperity. They will play a crucial role in addressing human capital issues such as future education, future skills, gender equality, research and development, innovation, entrepreneurship, and employment.

By involving various stakeholders and addressing key issues, the survey aims to create an action plan and vision document that will guide India's development and progress towards achieving its goals by 2047.

To create a transparent and inclusive National Education Policy document, the Ministry of Education (MoE, formerly known as the Ministry of Human Resource Development or MHRD) engaged in an extensive process of deliberations and consultations with stakeholders, including the public. Over 2 lakh suggestions were gathered from 2.5 lakh gram panchayats, 6,600 blocks, 6,000 urban local bodies, and 676 districts. This collaborative effort resulted in formulating the Draft NEP-2019, which was made available on the MHRD's website and the 'MyGov Innovate' portal to gather views from stakeholders (PIB). After several iterations, the NEP-2020 was officially launched on 29 July 2020.

The NEP-2020 acknowledges the importance of preparing for the demographic dividend and cultivating a skilled workforce with multidisciplinary abilities to tackle various challenges such as scientific and technological advancements, climate change, pollution, depleting resources, and the emergence of epidemics and pandemics. The policy emphasises a shift towards a system that prioritises critical thinking, problem-solving, and holistic learning by focusing on content.

To address these challenges, the NEP-2020 has proposed a range of reforms, including equitable access to high-quality education, integration of multidisciplinary and holistic education with skill development, promotion of research excellence, fostering critical and creative thinking, establishing strong connections with the Indian Knowledge System (IKS), and reinstating teachers as respected and essential members of society. The policy also highlights the importance of institutional autonomy, technology integration, internationalisation of higher education, governance and regulatory restructuring, multidisciplinary curricula, blended pedagogy, and reliable assessment methods.

Given that education is a concurrent subject, the successful implementation of NEP-2020 requires collaborative efforts between the central and state governments. To facilitate this collaboration, the MoE engaged actively with various ministries, departments, State and Union Territory governments, and regulatory bodies involved in

state open schools and providing equitable and quality education from the foundational stage to grade level.
- **Webinars**: The NIOS organised webinars with state open schools to promote and expand the open schooling system in India.
- **Translation of Courses**: Courses related to the Indian knowledge tradition and Sanskrit literature were translated into English medium and uploaded at the secondary and senior secondary levels.
- **Gender Inclusion**: NEP-2020 provides for the Gender Inclusion Fund (GIF) to support girls and transgender students. The Department of School Education and Literacy has incorporated interventions for girls in its schemes, such as free textbooks, hostels, stipends, and self-defence training.
- **Jadui Pitara**: In February 2023, NCERT launched *Jadui Pitara*, a play-based learning-teaching material for three to eight-year-old children. It includes playbooks, toys, puzzles, posters, flashcards, storybooks, and worksheets designed to cater to the diverse needs of learners in the foundational stage.
- **PARAKH (The National Assessment Centre)**: Set up under NCERT, PARAKH brings school boards across states and UTs on a common assessment platform. It focuses on improving the assessment system in line with NEP-2020.

The UGC introduced significant initiatives, including regulations on the Academic Bank of Credits, multiple entry and exit in academic programmes, Common Universities Entrance Test (CUET), and Online and Open and Distance Learning (ODL) Education. These initiatives promote online education, enhance flexibility in academic programmes, and facilitate the seamless movement of students across the education system.

The UGC also launched guidelines for internship/apprenticeship-embedded degree programmes, internationalisation of higher education, establishing research and development cells in HEIs, and conferring autonomous status on colleges. These guidelines and regulations encourage practical learning, global exposure, research focus, and autonomy for colleges.

Furthermore, the UGC has introduced the Four Year Undergraduate Programme (FYUP) to provide students with greater flexibility in choosing their areas of study. It has also implemented the National Credit Framework (NCrF) and the National Higher Education Qualifications Framework (NHEQF) to facilitate credit transfer and define learning outcomes for graduates.

To strengthen industry-academia collaboration, the UGC has launched guidelines on Professor of Practice, allowing industry experts and professionals to serve as guest faculty in universities and colleges. Additionally, measures have been taken to address students' grievances through the UGC Grievance Redressal Regulations.

The AICTE, on the other hand, has focused on promoting technical education in regional languages and ensuring practical exposure for students. It has permitted engineering courses in eight regional languages and organised awareness workshops and conferences to facilitate internships for students. The AICTE internship portal has been strengthened to provide more internship opportunities, and AICTE-IDEA Labs have been established to promote new-age learning and hands-on experience. AICTE has framed the course curriculum for the introduction of IKS in technical education. Students completing 18-20 credits in IKS are eligible for a minor degree in the subject.

The AICTE has also collaborated with industry partners for faculty development programmes in emerging areas and launched the National Educational Alliance for Technology (NEAT) Cell for skilling and reskilling. Emphasis has been given to the importance of education in the mother tongue and regional languages, offering degree programmes in different languages. Translation tools have also been provided.

The MoE organised the Akhil Bharatiya Shiksha Samagam (ABSS) from 7 to 9 July 2022. It provided a platform for eminent academicians, policymakers, and academic leaders to deliberate on and share their experiences and discuss the road map for the effective implementation of NEP-2020. The event was organised as part of the capacity-building of academic, administrative, and institutional leaders from universities (central, state, deemed, and private), and Institutes of National Importance (IIT, IIM, NIT, IISER) from all over the country. Various stakeholders presented the progress of the implementation of NEP in their respective institutions and also shared noteworthy strategies, best practices, and success stories.

The key takeaways of ABSS 2022 were:
- Resolve to work collectively for transforming India into an equitable and vibrant knowledge society.
- Establish India as a knowledge-based superpower and prepare students for the challenges of the twenty-first century.
- Develop forward-looking, world-class institutions that work on the principle of Student First-Teacher Led learning.

- Adopt good practices from better performing universities to improve the ecosystem of other universities. Towards this, the practice of 'Learn from thy neighbour' should be the motto.
- Develop India as a hub of research and innovation and work on solutions for climate change, technology creation for waste-to-wealth for promotion of a circular economy.
- Follow the principles of good governance, accountability and transparency; work towards accreditation; improved ranking and promotion of India as an attractive global destination for education.
- Develop a roadmap for 'lab to land' and use the experience of ground realities and traditional experience in the labs.
- Promote gender parity and address the needs of socially and educationally disadvantaged groups.
- Create better learning opportunities using digital resources for a wider audience on affordable and equitable basis with lifelong learning orientation.

Implementation of NEP through Consultation and Collaboration

The implementation of the NEP-2020 is being carried out through consultation and collaboration among multiple bodies and stakeholders. The MoE, Central Advisory Board of Education (CABE), State/UT governments, education-related ministries, State departments of education, boards, National Testing Agency (NTA), regulatory bodies of schools and Higher Education Institutions (HEIs), the National Council of Educational Research and Training (NCERT), State Councils of Educational Research and

Training (SCERTs), schools, and HEIs are all involved in implementing the policy.

To facilitate the implementation process, the Department of School Education & Literacy developed an indicative and suggestive NEP implementation plan for school education, and of Students' and Teachers' Holistic Advancement through Quality Education (SARTHAQ). This plan focuses on defining activities with clear goals, outcomes, and timeframes. It assists states, UTs, and other organisations in implementing the goals and objectives of NEP-2020.

In the Department of Higher Education, actionable activities have been grouped under nine themes, which include:
- Multidisciplinary and holistic education,
- Equity and inclusion,
- Research, innovation and ranking,
- Global outreach of higher education,
- Motivated, energised and capable faculty,
- Integrated higher education system,
- Governance and regulation,
- Indigenous Knowledge Systems (IKS), languages, culture and values, and
- Technology: use and integration.

The UGC and AICTE have formed expert groups and sub-groups to work on these themes, identifying outputs and implementing agencies along with timelines.

The Department of School Education and Literacy has constituted subject/theme-wise committees to address various recommendations of NEP-2020.

These committees, under the bureau head and heads of concerned autonomous bodies, are working on topics like toy-based pedagogy, Early Childhood Care and Education

(ECCE), and expanding the scope of the Teacher Eligibility Test (TET).

A review committee was also constituted to review the implementation of NEP-2020, chaired by Dr K Kasturirangan. In addition, NEP-2020 provides for establishing a Gender Inclusion Fund (GIF) dedicated to girls and transgender students, aiming to provide equitable quality education. The Department has incorporated interventions for girls in the Samagra Shiksha Scheme, including free textbooks and uniforms, residential schools and hostels, transport and escort facilities, aids and appliances for children with special needs, upgrading Kasturba Gandhi Balika Vidyalayas (KGBVs) to provide residential and schooling facilities up to Class 12, stipends for Children With Special Needs (CWSN), girls, besides incinerator and sanitary pad vending machines in girls' hostels, and self-defence training for girls in government schools.

Karnataka was the first state to launch NEP 2020 on 23 August 2021. The State government introduced various initiatives such as integrating online courses into degree programmes, revising college curricula, offering multiple programmes, collaborating with foreign universities for student exchange programmes, promoting interdisciplinary courses, and emphasising sports education. Overall, the implementation of NEP-2020 involves multiple stakeholders, coordination among various bodies, and the development of plans, committees, and expert groups to ensure a synchronised and systematic approach to achieve the policy's objectives (PIB).

NEP 2020 Implementation Challenges

Despite these initiatives, the implementation of NEP-

2020 in India faces issues that need to be addressed for its successful execution. Some of these problems and their possible solutions are as follows:

Inadequate funding: According to Prof. Philip G Altbach, research professor and distinguished fellow, Center for International Higher Education, Boston College, United States, Indian higher education, at both the State and Central levels, has been dramatically underfunded for decades. The expansion of the education system in recent years, particularly in colleges, without direct government funding, has further strained the resources. Prof. N. V. Varghese, former Vice-Chancellor, NIEPA in his essay on NEP-2020, *Implications for Planning for Implementation in Higher Education* (Mittal, 2022), writes that unless the implementing institutions are revitalised or new institutions are created with adequate financial and human resources, the very many ideas contained in the policy may remain at the ideation level only. To translate these ideas into operational practices, new energy needs to be created in the system through improving the effectiveness of existing institutions. To overcome this, significant investment is required from both the universities and the government. The NEP-2020 emphasises the need for increased public investment in education, and states that the Central and State Governments should work together to achieve the target of 6 per cent of GDP for the education sector.

Revitalisation of Institutions: The implementation of the NEP-2020 requires that existing institutions are revitalised and new institutions with adequate financial and human resources be established. Policy ideas by themselves are not enough; the effectiveness of institutions must be improved and policy ideas be translated into operational practices. This may involve restructuring existing institutions, providing training and support to faculty, and promoting a culture of innovation and research.

Quality of Faculty: To enhance the quality of education, it is crucial to invest in faculty development programmes, attract and retain talented individuals, and provide them with opportunities for professional growth. This can be achieved through continuous professional development of faculty through training programmes, research collaborations, and incentives for excellence in teaching and research.

Curriculum Flexibility: The NEP-2020 acknowledges the need for a more flexible, adaptable, and student-centric curriculum. To address this, curriculum reforms must be undertaken to promote interdisciplinary learning, skill development, and industry relevance. This requires consultations with stakeholders, including industry experts and academia, to design curricula that meet the evolving and emerging needs of the job market.

Internationalisation and Research Focus: The NEP-2020 aims to enhance international mobility and promote research and innovation in HEIs. However, the current scenario faces challenges in terms of low international mobility and a paucity of research-focused institutions. To overcome these obstacles, efforts have to be made to forge collaborations with foreign universities, establish research centres of excellence, and provide support for international exposure and research opportunities to students and faculty.

Digital Learning: The Covid-19 pandemic highlighted the importance of digital learning, but in India, this area needs further investment. To bridge the digital divide and ensure access to quality education for all, the NEP-2020 emphasises the need for digital infrastructure and online learning platforms. This requires investment in technology, training of teachers for effective online teaching, and creating a conducive environment for digital learning.

***Collaboration and Stakeholder Engagement*:** The successful implementation of the NEP-2020 relies on the collective engagement and participation of various stakeholders, including the Central and State governments, educational institutions, teachers, students, and parents. For effective policy implementation, regular consultations, coordination, and collaboration among these stakeholders are essential. Clear communication, capacity building, and continuous monitoring and evaluation are also crucial for the smooth execution of the policy.

The FICCI Higher Education in India: Vision 2047 released in November 2022 summarises the enhancing of the student experience and ensuring that learners are supported by operators across the ecosystem. This is imperative for the development of Indian higher education.

The Way Forward

In conclusion, while the NEP-2020 provides a comprehensive vision for transforming the education system in India, the challenges and issues in its implementation need to be addressed urgently. That requires sustained commitment, collaboration, and investment from all stakeholders. It requires the collective engagement and participation of the Central and various State Governments and their educational institutions. All the facets of the NEP-2020 and their implementation strategies and action plans require careful and rigorous deliberation and cohesion. This is imperative for ensuring implementation in a systematic and phased manner with emphasis on key areas and proactively addressing possible bottlenecks.

By focusing on student-centric approaches, enhancing research and innovation, developing faculty, promoting internationalisation, investing in digital learning, and ensuring adequate funding, the implementation of NEP-2020 can be effectively realised.

Bibliography

AICTE. https://free.aicte-india.org.

Chandra, Pankaj. (2017). *Building Universities That Matter*, New Delhi: Orient Blackswan Private Limited.

Chandrasekhar, S. (1991). *Truth and Beauty*, New Delhi: Penguin Books India (P) Ltd.

Delors, Jacques. (1996). *Learning the Treasure Within*, Paris: UNESCO Publishing, Paris.

Einstein, Albert. (1954). *Ideas and Opinions*, New Delhi: Rupa and Co. FICCI-EY-Report. (2022). *Higher Education in India: Vision 2047*, November 2022. https://www.ficci-hes.com/FICCI-EY-Report.pdf

Gandhi, M.K. (2016). *India of My Dreams*, Ahmedabad: Navajivan Mudralaya Publishing House.

Harari, Yuval Noah. (2018). *21 Lessons from the 21st Century*, 2018, Vintage, Printed and bound in India by Thomson Press India Ltd.

https://theprint.in/india/ugc-chairman-reviews-progress-of-nep-2020-with-vice-chancellors-of-45-central-varsities/1371249/

https://www.youtube.com/live/PtX1kaaMqnw?feature=share

Kara, Shyna. (2021). 'Covid lesson for teachers: How teaching-learning methods evolved during pandemic,' *The Indian Express*, February 6, 2021. Kothari, D.S. (2000). *Education and Character Building*, New Delhi:

National Institute of Scientific Communication.

Kripalani, J.B. (2005). *Gandhi His Life and Thought*, New Delhi: Publications Division, Ministry of I & B, Government of India.

Ministry of Human Resource Development (MHRD). (2020). *National Policy on Education, 2020* (NEP-2020), New Delhi: Government of India.

Mittal, Pankaj and Sistla Rama Devi Pani. Eds. (2022). *Implementing National Policy-2020. A Roadmap*. ISBN: 81-7520-162-2, November 2022, New Delhi: Association of Indian Universities.

Naik, J.P. (1997). *The Education Commission and After*, New Delhi: Efficient Offset Printers.

NCERT (2000). National Curriculum Framework for School Education, New Delhi: NCERT.

PIB https:// static. pib. go v. in/ Write Read Data/ userfiles/ f ile/ NEPBookletFinalFO2Z.pdf

PIB, September 7 (2021). https://pib.gov.in/PressReleasePage.aspx?PRID=1752827.

PIB 09 July 2022 https://pib.gov.in/PressReleaseIframePage.aspx?PRID=1840409.

PIB MAY 22, 2023 pib.gov.in/PressReleaseIframePage.aspx?

PRID=1926438

Radhakrishnan, S. (1990). *Radhakrishnan Reader: An Anthology*. Edited by K.M. Munshi et al. New Delhi: Bhartiya Vidya Bhavan.

Rajput, J.S. (2001). 'Optimizing Institutional Functioning', in *Experiences in School Education*. Edited by J.S. Rajput et al. New Delhi: NCERT.

Rajput, J.S. (2016). *Indian Education in Times of Global Change*, Delhi: Shipra Publications.

Rajput, J.S. (2022). Hurdles in Excellence in Higher Education, *The Pioneer*, 2 May 2022, New Delhi.

Saiyidain, K.G. (2015). 'Universities and Intellectual Freedom', In: *A Life in Education*, edited by Zakiya Saiyidain Zaheer and Sayeda Saiyidain Hameed, New Delhi: Pan Macmillan.

Swami Tathagatananda. (2013). *Albert Einstein and his Human Side*, New York: Vedanta Society of New York.

Swami Vivekananda. *Complete Works of Swami Vivekananda*, Kolkata: Advaita Ashrama.

SWAYAM. https://swayam.gov.in/nc_details/NIOS.

UNICEF. https://www.unicef.org/rosa/documents/india-case-study World Bank. https://blogs.worldbank.org/education/reopening-schools-when-where-and-how).